Scrapbook Storytelling

Save family stories and memories with photos, journaling and your own creativity

Joanna Campbell Slan

Cover and inside pages:
Photography and design:
VIP Graphics
St. Louis, MO
(314) 535-1117

Scrapbook Storytelling: Save family stories and memories with photos, journaling and your own creativity.

03   02   01   00   5   4   3

Library of Congress Catalog Card Number 99-62201

ISBN: 0-9630222-8-8

First Edition. Printed and bound in the United States of America.

Production Team:
Editorial manager: Susan Todd, EFG, Inc.

Proofreading: Robert Saigh, Razorsharp
Communications, Inc., St. Louis, MO

Publisher:
EFG, Inc. — *The Elaine Floyd Group*
(314) 353-6100; fax (314) 353-1272
http://www.scrapbookstorytelling.com

The Elaine Floyd Group

Distributed to the trade by:
Betterway Books & North Light Books
Imprints of F&W Publications
1507 Dana Ave., Cincinnati, OH 45207
(800) 289-0963; fax: (513) 531-4082

PHYLLIS & MANNY CAPLIN 1983

This book is
dedicated to
Emmanuel Caplin,
whose memory is a
blessing.
. H .

Contents

Introduction
Hi!

Every summer of my childhood, my mother, sisters and I traveled to Summerville, South Carolina, to see my maternal grandmother. For hours we would sit on the porch and listen to Grandma's stories of our illustrious ancestors. Tales of Arthur Middleton, my great, great grandfather and signer of the Declaration of Independence. Tales of Grandma's courtship and how she and my grandfather celebrated the Armistice and their honeymoon, leaning out a window of the Chicago Palmer House and cheering with the crowds.

The stories I heard about my ancestors gave me courage. As I walked through my grandmother's dining room, the eyes of the ancestors looked down from their portraits, encouraging me and asking, "Who are you? How will you make us proud?"

*Figure I-1—***My Grandmother's House.** Southerners call a wide front porch like this a "piazza" (pee'-ah-zah). Here we would sit in rocking chairs as my grandmother told me wonderful stories about our family. The house is now called the Summerville Manigault house.

An Unbroken Circle

None of us stands alone but as a continuation of a long line of others. We are supported by our heritage, our families and our experiences. In an age of rapid change, our family stories take on increasing importance. Families often ask, "Who are we? What do we value? How do we feel about each other?" Our children turn to us to tell them the answers to these questions.

Of course, your photos will help tell part of the story but only a part. Until recently, photography was expensive. Today with the advent of simple and inexpensive photography, most of us find ourselves with a box, a drawer or a closet full of photos. That's wonderful, because the photos are a terrific starting point for capturing family stories. But they are just a "starting point." Photos in and of themselves are not the entire story.

Imagine for a moment, a rock strikes you in the head and you lose your memory. Would those photos still have meaning? Yes, you might still have that picture of Grandpa and his Model A, but what was Grandpa like?

Photos are one piece of the family mosaic. The other piece is the story. This book will help you become excited about the storytelling process, guide you through the writing process and share valuable scrapbooking tips along the way.

Who Can Use this Book

Teens: At this confusing time in life, scrapbooks offer a private place to share your feelings and changing relationships. (By committing your thoughts to paper, you'll be able to make better decisions and feel more in control of your life.)

Parents: Scrapbooks offer us the opportunity to share what matters most to us and to hold on to family memories. By sharing family stories, generations feel a sense of connectedness. Scrapbooks are one tool for bringing an entire family together while respecting our unique viewpoints.

> "...I have grandchildren now. For them, I feel a greater urgency to do what I can to convey the knowledge that our future as human beings depends upon our caring more for one another..."
>
> **—Lois Lowry**

Figure I-2—**The 13 Colonies**. This project shows how my son used scrapbook techniques and supplies for a school project. Scrapbooking offers children many tools for visual expression. By using archival quality paper and supplies, your child's project can be enjoyed for years to come.

Grandparents: When you scrapbook your life and your relationships, your grandchildren come to understand you in a new light. When you scrapbook your grandchildren, you come to understand them in a new light. Scrapbooks help close the gap created by years, generational differences and geographic distance.

Family historians: Every family has that wonderful person or two who is the keeper of the family history. Scrapbooking gives you new ways to display and share your family's story.

Teachers: Scrapbooking turns abstract concepts into vivid images. Encouraging young people to scrapbook their lives helps them view themselves as authors of their destiny. Scrapbooking helps students develop their interviewing skills, writing skills and organization skills. For the student who is a poor or reluctant writer, scrapbooking can offer great encouragement by combining artistic skills with journalism skills. For the student who is not artistic, scrapbooking encourages visual expression.

Art teachers: Because of the wealth of scrapbooking materials, it's easy to be creative with scrapbooks. Since one page will never be enough, the art teacher who introduces a child to scrapbooking helps a student start on a life-long involvement in art.

Scouting leaders: Scrapbooking helps scouts review their accomplishments over the year. As a den, pack or troop goes on year after year, a scrapbook helps scouts identify with the role of scouting in a changing world.

Librarians: By helping students scrapbook as they read, librarians teach the translation of words into images. When a student is directed to a historical event, scrapbooking can encourage the student to interview others, look up art, organize information and draw conclusions. Scrapbooks allow people to create

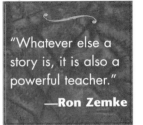

"Whatever else a story is, it is also a powerful teacher."
—**Ron Zemke**

Figure I-3—**Great Big Brownie Smile**. See that Great Big Brownie Smile on my face? If you don't have a photo of your child in uniform, take a photo of the uniform and add an age-appropriate photo of your child. Or just use a photo of your child and symbols of the organization. Notice the color copy of my badge sash that fits in the pocket.

Religious leaders: Scrapbooks give us a place to illustrate and save our spiritual and inward journey in an outward and physical way. For young people, a scrapbook can chronicle a child's introduction to faith. For adults, a scrapbook can be a sacred place that holds our questions and God's answers.

Business owners: A business scrapbook helps organizations define who they are, why they do what they do and what they value. Family business expert Mike Henning recommends showing the business scrapbook to new employees to give them a sense of history and values. By working together on a scrapbook, employees participate in an important team-building exercise.

Builders: A scrapbook of the building process details the journey from "a hole in the ground" to a "castle," creating a memorable gift. An album of photos helps buyers translate blueprints into reality.

Gardeners: By scrapbooking your garden, you preserve all the seasons and all the dreams. The next generation can see what you did and what you loved (see Figure 8-1, page 92).

By now, you could probably share your own list of people who might benefit from learning to tell their stories through scrapbooking. Making the invisible journey of our lives visible helps us see how far we've come and anticipate where we are going. As we use our talents and insights to record our lives, we blaze a trail for the next generation, a trail marked with signs of love.

*Figure I-4—***Soccer It to Me**. When my husband reported a funny conversation between Michael and his friend Josh, I scribbled the dialogue down in a notebook. Months later, I put together this page, Soccer It to Me. If you can capture key phrases, words and ideas, you'll be scrapbook storytelling before you know it.

SAGE PAGE

Where Do I Begin?

When my sister Margaret first introduced me to "modern" scrapbooking, I was overwhelmed. I wandered through the scrapbooking store looking at paper, embellishments, templates, adhesives and markers, but I didn't have the faintest idea what I— or anyone else—would do with all that junk. I bought one sheet. Big whoop. (I'm making up for lost time today. And it's not JUNK, it's critical to my art!)

I realized I needed a push to get my fanny out of the starting blocks. So, I attended organized sessions on scrapbooking. In order of value, here's what helped:

1. Attend Creative Memories crops. At my first crop, I sat immobilized for at least half an hour. Everyone else was merrily cropping and gluing and matting, and, gee whiz, I felt so stupid.

Yet, if I had it all to do over again, I wouldn't change a thing. If you've never scrapbooked, find the closest Creative Memories consultant and ask about attending a crop. These consultants will take you from zero to 60 in no time. Most consultants bring to the crop a wealth of supplies, equipment and samples. Their products are all archival quality, so you don't have to worry about reading labels.

2. Sign up for classes at scrapbooking specialty stores. The classes I've attended at scrapbook stores have been excellent. If you want to learn more about a specific skill, such as punch art or stenciling, they are particularly valuable. Don't be shy about asking questions. If you are stumped, you probably are not alone. We all have to start somewhere. Be sure to allow time before or after the class to wander around the store, look at products and make purchases.

3. Take classes offered by local craft stores. Here you will learn, in addition to some scrapbooking basics, how to use art products not yet in general use by the scrapbooking world.

What I'd Do Differently Today

1. Ask the qualifications of the person teaching the class. Don't look for a PhD in graphic arts, but do expect to hear some indication that this person has spent time learning scrapbooking skills. Listen for key words such as "well-organized," "creative," "helpful," and "knowledgeable."

2. Ask if the instructor will allow participants time to share their pages, especially if the class isn't focused on learning a specific skill. Often we learn as much from a fellow participant as we do from the instructor.

3. Ask what supplies or equipment you need to bring and what will be provided. Make sure to mark your "stuff" clearly with your name.

4. Ask if there will be handouts. A handout gives you something to write on and take home.

5. Ask what the class cancellation and no-show policies are. If the class does not fill, will they automatically cancel? If your child comes home from school with a temperature of 102 degrees, will you lose your class fee?

6. Ask if there will be any special offers the night of the class. You may want to postpone buying that circle-cutter until after the circle-cutter class. The more you learn about equipment, the more particular you will be about what you buy.

1 Catching Your Life's Stories

When my son, Michael, was seven, he began to have nightmares. "At this age," droned a doctor in a parenting book, "the child realizes that bad things can happen to him. His young mind is busy with possibilities."

Night after night, my husband and I would awaken to cries from the bedroom across the hall. Wearily, we took turns stumbling through the dark to our son's side. Then one day when Michael and I were out shopping, we wandered into a Native American store. From the ceiling hung an intricate dream catcher. The small tag on the dream catcher explained that Native Americans believed you could depend on a dream catcher to catch and hold your dreams while you slept. A thought buzzed through my head, and I whisked Michael to the local craft store. There we bought sequins and beads and a metal hoop. That night he and I made a dream catcher, and we hung it over his bed, directly above his pillow. For the first time in many nights, our family slept quietly all night long.

My scrapbook is a *story catcher*. My life swirls around me. When I try to grasp life, it slithers and slides right through my fingers. So, instead of grabbing at life, I coax it into my scrapbook.

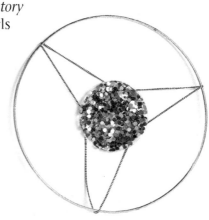

Figure 1-1—**The Dream Catcher** that Michael and I made hangs over his bed today to ward off bad dreams.

Catching Your Life's Stories

This book was designed to help you hold time in a bottle. You can capture your daily life—and even your past—on the pages of your scrapbook. While you'll want to include holidays, special events and rites of passage, I'll show you ways to expand your scrapbooking to include life's sacred but ordinary moments.

We live in a time where the stories we see and hear in the media seem to have more importance than the stories of our lives. Inadvertently, we are telling our children, "The people on television and in the media have lives we want you to emulate." By taking the time to scrapbook, we are teaching our children, our families and ourselves to pay attention to what really matters to us. We decide which of our stories are worth keeping. We decide what makes headlines. We become the heroes whose great deeds we celebrate.

As individuals we may never make the front of the local paper, but we are special. We are the fiber from which our country is woven. With this in mind, you'll want to scrapbook daily challenges, rewards, ups and downs, funny stuff, friendships, places, activities, bright spots and your reactions to moments of history.

Once upon a time, scrapbooks were filled with scraps of paper, ticket stubs, pictures cut from magazines and stodgy planned photo portraits. Today, scrapbooks are homes for scraps of your life. Photos, stories, memorabilia and paper combine together to tell who you are and what you value.

Reasons to Catch Your Stories

Many people begin a scrapbook because they are concerned about preserving their precious family photos. They mourn over the images destroyed by magnetic photo albums, poor storage and non-archival papers. These folks turn to scrapbooking as a state-of-the-art way to preserve important photographs and documents. This book will show you new ways to tell the stories that give meaning to your important photographs and documents.

Others want to preserve family history for the next generation. During our lifetimes, we've lost

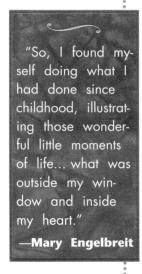

"So, I found myself doing what I had done since childhood, illustrating those wonderful little moments of life... what was outside my window and inside my heart."

—Mary Engelbreit

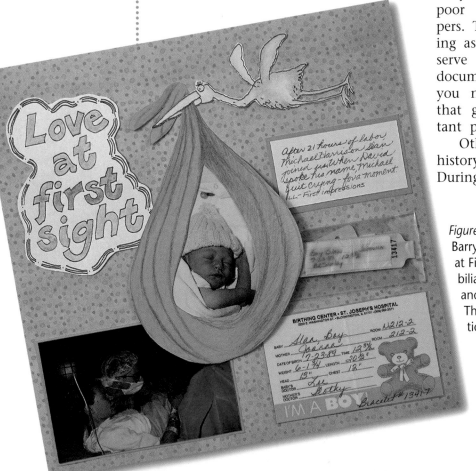

*Figure 1-2—**Love at First Sight***. When Dr. Barry Slotky handed us our son, it was Love at First Sight. This page preserves memorabilia, the hospital tag for Michael's crib and his arm bracelet, in acid- free plastic. The stork was copied from a congratulations card we received.

family members, we've seen events and changes that color our outlook on life, and we want our children and grandchildren to know what we know. Inside this book, you'll see new techniques for creating heritage pages (family history pages or pages featuring older black and white photos) and "time capsule" pages that show how the past relates to the present.

Some people start scrapbooking as a gift to leave their children, a record of the love they have for their families. This book will serve as an inspiring guide for you, teaching you to tell your story, helping you to see important life moments and giving you new ideas for pages.

Still others fall in love with scrapbooking when they see how quickly their children grow and how easily tender moments are forgotten. Because of the journalistic principles underlying this book, you'll become better at documenting important aspects of your children's lives.

For those who love the crafts aspect of scrapbooking—the cutting and pasting and creating beautiful art—this book has new ideas, techniques and creative combinations you'll want to try. Last but not least, for those who enjoy the social aspects of scrapbooking, sometimes called "quilting for the millennium," why not call a few friends and use this book as an excuse to schedule a crop? ("Crops" are super-scrapbooking sessions.)

What Exactly Is Scrapbook Storytelling?

Typically when you hear the word "story," you might think of a fairy tale or an anecdote. That's not what we mean. Here's our definition of a story:

Story — Any account of events or happenings.

A story can be as simple as one sentence or as complex as a book. A complete story might include all the aspects of information (who, what, when, where and why), whereas a scaled down version of a story might only elaborate on one

"If I could save time in a bottle..."
—**Jim Croce**

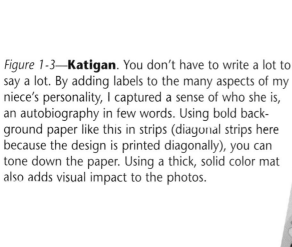

Figure 1-3—**Katigan**. You don't have to write a lot to say a lot. By adding labels to the many aspects of my niece's personality, I captured a sense of who she is, an autobiography in few words. Using bold background paper like this in strips (diagonal strips here because the design is printed diagonally), you can tone down the paper. Using a thick, solid color mat also adds visual impact to the photos.

"The passports that brought great-grandparents to this country, the old letters from the attic trunk, the yellowed diaries—they give a flavor of those from whom we have sprung. In every reunion the old ones should have a chance to speak briefly about their past and also to voice their hopes for the family's future."

—Alex Haley

of the aspects. Every item that exists has a story attached to it—how it came to be, why it exists and who bought it. The purpose of family stories is to share who we are and what we value. Stories give important background about photos, memorabilia and keepsakes, explaining why one person's trash is another person's treasure.

Since many of life's wonderful moments are never captured on film, you probably have stories that belong in your scrapbook but don't have corresponding photographs. That's why these pages also share new ideas for scrapbooking those unrepresented but important moments. You don't need photos to tell a story, but you do need stories to tell. A storytelling scrapbook will help you capture what is in your heart and transfer your life onto paper.

Take the Scrapbook Test

Is your current level of journaling sufficient? Are you telling family stories or are you putting photos in an album?

Here's the test: Hand your scrapbook to someone you like who doesn't know you well. What do the pages tell them about you and your family? Do you find yourself jumping in and explaining your pages? What would happen if you weren't around to tell the story?

Here's another test: If you had to give your scrapbook to family members right now, would they know how much you love them? I like to think of my scrapbook as a long, illustrated love letter I'm leaving behind for my family.

By the way, these tests are hard to pass. But think of it... someday your scrapbook will have to tell your stories without you. Your scrapbook can be more than a photo album, it can be a memory album, an illustrated journal of your heart, if you work with the principles in this book.

*Figure 1-4—***Star-Struck***. This before-and-after set shows how scrapbook storytelling pages differ from ordinary pages. The headline and the embellishments on the first page (left) don't add any new information. On the scrapbook storytelling page (right), the journaling and embellishments tell the story of my mother's desire to become a professional dancer. The memorabilia also supports the theme of my mother's career.

What Keeps Us from Telling Stories

Let's face it. We love those photos of our kids and kin. We want to preserve the memories that flood back when we look at the faces peering out at us from the image in our hands. Putting those photos in an album is neat, too. We feel a sense of accomplishment as we line up one album page after another and that shoebox of photos empties out. But writing? Who wants to do that?

You know you should. Then, you wonder what will you write? What if you make a mistake and mess up the whole page? What if you misspell a word? What if people can't read your handwriting?

Here are 15 common reasons why people find writing in scrapbooks difficult. See if these strike a chord with you:

1. Once upon a time you were told you can't write. Now you get a knot in your stomach when you have to write a grocery list.

2. You don't know what to say. You draw a blank. Yours is a classic case of writer's block.

3. You usually don't leave room on the page for writing.

4. You are worried about committing the words to the scrapbook. You are afraid you will ruin the page you just spent hours laying out and pasting down.

5. You are afraid of having a misspelling or a grammatical error.

6. The situation in the photos brings up unresolved feelings for you. You waffle between being honest and being cute. Exactly who is going to see this scrapbook, anyway?

7. You don't know where to start. You know what you want to say, but you aren't sure how to say it.

8. Your handwriting is awful. No one will be able to read it and you'll mess up a great page.

> "Storytelling is a psalm of praise and thanksgiving for the love and connection of family. Stories are the heart and soul of our culture. They give us hope and help us set goals for ourselves."
>
> **—Eileen Silva Kindig**

Figure 1-5—
Busy as Beavers. This could easily be used as a family holiday letter. The beaver was color copied from a magazine ad. To correct a misspelling that I made in a name, I cut out the offending letters with a craft knife and covered the back of the hole I made with a scrap of the same paper. I cut apart and switched the offending letters and glued the letters back down correctly.

9. Scrapbooking is fun; writing is work.

10. You're worried you'll be wrong about what you document. What if you call that snarly looking woman Aunt Sally and it's really Grand-Aunt Sue?

11. You would like to write (honest), but you don't have a photo that illustrates what you'd like to write about or the photo you have is awful, so why write about it?

12. One picture is worth a thousand words, right? What could you possibly add to make the photo more meaningful?

13. These aren't your family photos. You married them. You not only aren't sure what to write, you aren't sure who these people are. (We received a Christmas card this year complete with photo of a family we've never heard of! Guess we'd better call, eh?)

14. You can scrapbook at a cropping party, but you have to write alone. Scrapbooking is social, but writing is still a solitary pursuit. You can crop and talk, but when you write and talk, look out.

15. You'd like to write more, but you can't think of any details about the photos worth sharing.

If you felt a twinge at any of these questions, you've found the right book. With a little help, you'll become more enthusiastic about storytelling, learn new ways to make your written remarks look good, find ways to make writing easier than ever and discover lots of ways to cover up those inevitable mistakes.

What Is Journaling?

Scrapbookers call writing on pages "journaling," not to be confused with the true definition of journaling—to keep a diary. For scrapbookers, journaling entails adding written commentary to a page. From now on, we'll use journaling and writing interchangeably.

Figure 1-6—**Michael's First Menorah.** Journaling by hand is but one journaling option. While you may want to have samples of your handwriting in your album, dare to try other ways to capture your sentiments. Since working on this page I've discovered the joy of computer journaling with WordPerfect and a color printer. My journaling goes much faster, and I can get more words on the page.

How to Use This Book

This book offers you a variety of ways to find information.

❏ To improve your writing, read the book from front to back. If you find an unfamiliar term, see the Index (page 133) for its definition.

❏ For page ideas, just flip through the book and refer to the Page Chart (page 125) for techniques and supplies.

❏ For ideas about using a particular skill or supply turn to the Page Chart (page 125) to find which layouts feature which skills and supplies.

❏ To find tips, skim through the pages and look for the boxes labeled "tips."

❏ For supplies, take the Suppliers listing (page 131) to your local retailer, or call the suppliers to find your local retailer.

❏ To build your overall scrapbooking skills, check the Page Chart (page 125) where the pages are evaluated with a 1, 2 or 3, with 1 being the simplest and 3 being most complex. Please note that complexity is a mixture of how much time and effort a page takes *and* the amount of journaling it requires.

You'll note we've delineated three levels of storytelling: *Minimal journaling* would require the least amount of writing. *Intermediate* would use more writing and interviewing skills. *Extensive journaling* would require the most writing, interviewing and editing skills.

Above all, allow yourself to play in your scrapbook. As one woman said at a crop, "This is arts and crafts time for the big kids."

Tip!

Pooches aren't the only ones who need rewards. Start your scrapbooking efforts by purchasing the ultimate reward, the therapeutic size bag of M&Ms. (That's a whopping 10 ounces for those of you who are wondering.) Dole out as desired.

*Figure 1-7—***Tulips***Two Friends**. Curl Hansen took this picture of my friend Sharon Bowman and me at the annual Women's Conference he produces. (You gotta love a man who schedules a women's conference next to an outlet mall.) The centers of the big tulips were cut out to become frames for postcard images.

2 Preserving Family Values

Do you ever forget whether you've had lunch? Do you ever arrive home and wonder how you got there? Do you ever find yourself eating, drinking and working from your car while driving 65 miles per hour? Scrapbooking time is time to slow down. Savor each moment, one by one. Give yourself the gift of being present and fully available to the now.

Like most of the women I know, I want it all. The great news about scrapbooking is that when we scrapbook we can have and preserve it all.

Knowing that you plan to scrapbook an experience helps you "be in the moment." You can savor each experience more fully with the delicious anticipation of later enjoyment as well.

Instead of starting from a place of panic—in other words what photos do you have and when are you going to get them in an album?—start from a place of joy. What would you like to have? What is important that you preserve? What seemingly ordinary parts of your life make each day extraordinary and beautiful?

In other words, what should you scrapbook? What should you write about? What should you photograph?

Don't freak out when you hear people say, "I'm all caught up with my scrapbooks." The fact that you have photos waiting to go onto pages means you've got fun in your future! This isn't a race. As long as your photos aren't in any danger, take the time to sniff your markers—er—smell the flowers while you scrapbook.

Think Before You Create a Page

In the rush to create pages, most scrapbookers ignore the journaling. Instead, create pages that support the stories you want your children to own. View your photos as one source of the story. While preserving your family's photos, preserve the story, too. Your end result will be much more powerful.

When you think "story and values," you will plan your pages and themes to support those values you hold dear. You can best illustrate your story and values by continuing to scrapbook life's milestones and adding pages built around three main areas: your family, your times and yourself.

1. Your Family

The album filled with family photos stands as mute testimony of how alike and yet how different we all are.

The album's pages praise our daily efforts to get along, work side by side and grow into the best people we can be. Special occasions mark life's dreams, but day-to-day we live life's reality.

When we moved into this house five years ago, our son Michael's head was even with the countertops. He was always smacking his head on a counter. Today, at the ripe old age of nine, Michael has shot up to the height of my chin. Counter bonking is no longer a concern. Often I find myself wondering where did that little guy go?

We think we have forever with each other. That's not true. Our lives are as ethereal as the cottonwood seeds on the wind. The daily stuff of life cries out for our attention. Those seemingly insignificant moments between the "high points" are the truest, sweetest times we have.

> "It is Sunday night and my kids are willingly being held captive in the dining room. Gathered around the table, we are doing something so huge it almost takes my breath away: we are telling stories."
> —**Eileen Silva Kindig**

Figure 2-1—**Snow Much Fun**. Yesterday, as Michael tumbled off his sled and lay panting in the snow, he raised his fist in the air and shouted, "This is the best day of my life!" I felt a catch in my throat as I prayed, "Oh, I hope not, little man. I hope there is much more to come." But he made his point. What makes the music sweet is the space between the notes—the "ordinary" days that make up our lives.

The hill behind the Burnham pool was fast and slick. Kids had created a bump that caused your sled to hop into the air at the end. Michael spilled into the ground, raised both fists and yelled, "This is the best day of my life!"

Michael Slan   December 5, 1999

Possible daily scrapbooking titles and topics include (jot down any inspirations that come to mind):

❏ A Day in the Life of—every family member's typical day

✎ _____

❏ Weekend Activities—places to go, things to eat, people to visit

✎ _____

❏ Bedtime—clothes, habits, rituals

✎ _____

❏ Snow Days—digging out, no school, playtime

✎ _____

❏ Dinner at Our House—typical menus, where we sit, prayers, table settings

✎ _____

❏ Inside Jokes—jokes, funny lines, practical jokes, nicknames

✎ _____

❏ Bad Hair Days—if you dare!

✎ _____

❏ Family Funnies—those stories we share around the holidays that make us laugh and remember

✎ _____

❏ Family Myths—those stories we'll forget if someone doesn't write them down

✎ _____

❏ Worship—where we worship, how we worship and what we hold sacred

✎ _____

❏ Good Works—how our family serves others

✎ _____

❏ Chore Wars—jobs and workers

✎ _____

❏ Pets—outdoor and indoor animals we love

✎ _____

❏ Places—favorite haunts, movie theatres, shopping centers, grocery stores, historic sites

✎ _____

❏ Out to Eat—favorite restaurants and "the usual" orders you place

✎ _____

❏ Heigh-ho, Heigh-ho, It's Off to Work/School/the Mall We Go—the route, the stops and the players

✎ _____

❏ Nap-time—candid shots of nappers, their favorite locations and cover-ups

✎ _____

> "Families are families, after all, with warts and beauty marks unique to themselves."
> **—Dorothy Curran**

> "...Keep in mind one piece of advice as you scrapbook: the ordinary occurrences of life can make the best scrapbook pages of all!"
> **—Lisa Bearnson**

- ❑ Laundry Day—sorting the wash, dirty stuff, washing, folding, putting stuff away
  ✏ ____
- ❑ Mealtime Madness—making, eating and washing up
  ✏ ____
- ❑ Family Tree—who we are, where we came from, how we met
  ✏ ____
- ❑ Heritage Homage—our ethnic background, how we value old traditions, the reasons behind the traditions
  ✏ ____
- ❑ Roots—the extended family, where they live and how they are related
  ✏ ____

> "[Family stories that] are told and retold at family gatherings... are important to the sense of family... Stories aren't icing; they're basic ingredients in any group that claims to be family."
>
> —**Dolores Curran**

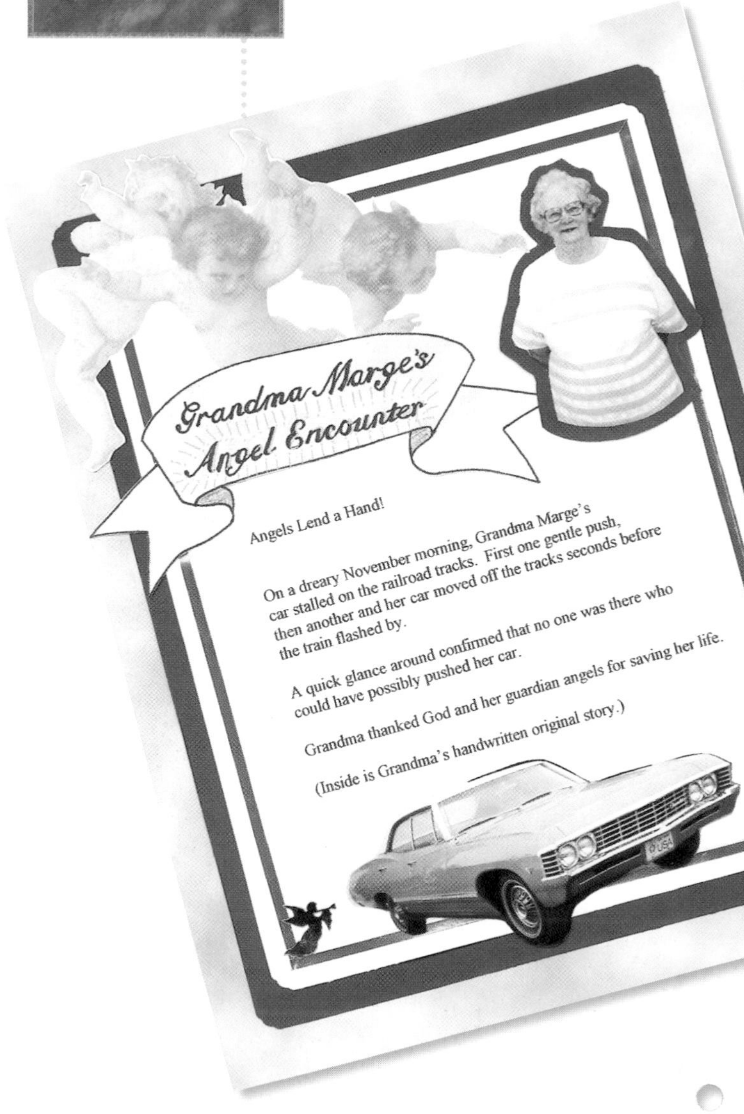
Grandma Marge's
Angel Encounter
Angels Lend a Hand!
On a dreary November morning, Grandma Marge's car stalled on the railroad tracks. First one gentle push, then another and her car moved off the tracks seconds before the train flashed by.
A quick glance around confirmed that no one was there who could have possibly pushed her car.
Grandma thanked God and her guardian angels for saving her life.
(Inside is Grandma's handwritten original story.)

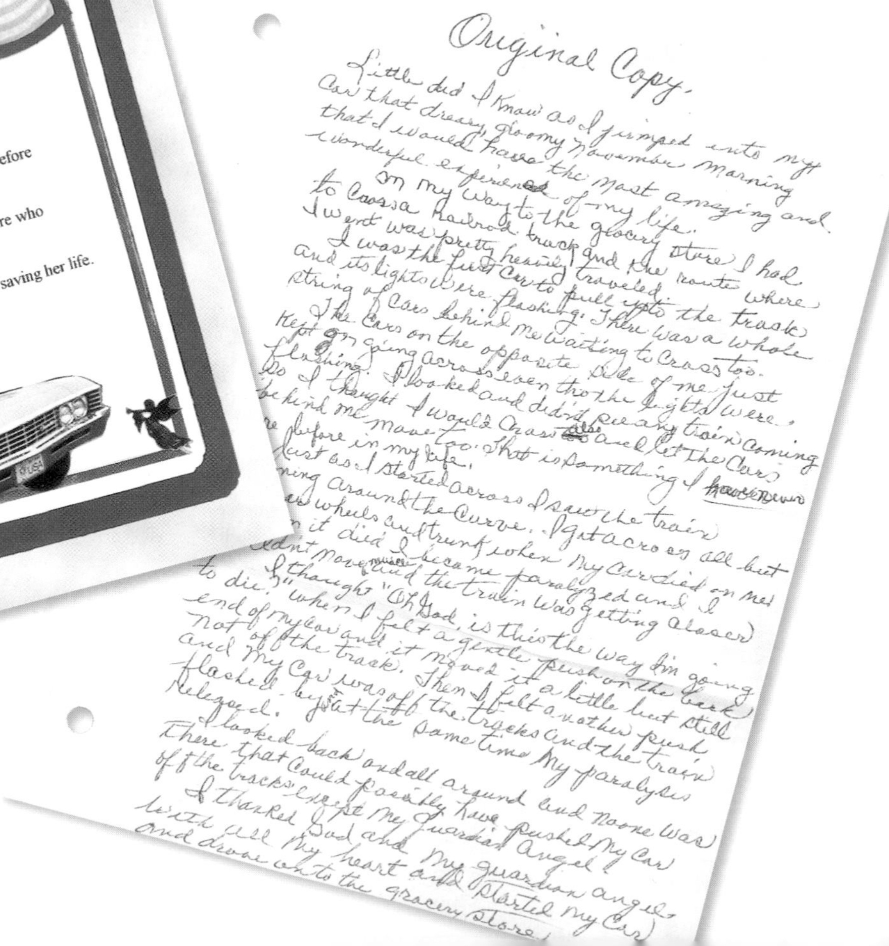
Original Copy.
Little did I know as I jumped into my car that dreary, gloomy November morning that I would have the most amazing and wonderful experience of my life.

Figure 2-2—**Angel Encounter**. Scrapbooks are the perfect place to save family stories. Grandma Marge's handwritten account of her angel encounter fits in a pocket inside the page. The photo of her and her car help tell the tale in detail.

2. Your Times

We all forget how quickly the world changes. We take so much for granted and we neglect to note it. Yet, world events help define us. They define the times we live in.

Ask any baby-boomer where he or she was when John F. Kennedy was shot. Ask this generation where they were when they heard that Princess Diana had died. Events are seared into our collective consciousness, yet we gloss over them.

Take the time to journal observations about the times you live in. Note how you see events, how you experienced them and how they touched your life. Comments about your times help give you a place in time and space. Such pages are useful for talking with your children about how the world has changed.

Think how exciting a scrapbook that includes information about Halley's Comet would be for a grandchild awaiting Halley's reapproach to Earth. Imagine the fascination a child might have with how your neighborhood changes. Share the import of the politics of our time. Your view may never, ever make the front pages of the local newspaper, but your view will make headlines in your family's daily journals.

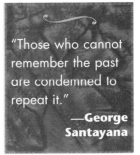

"Those who cannot remember the past are condemned to repeat it."
—**George Santayana**

Figure 2-3—**Goodbye, England's Rose**. We watched as her fairytale turned sour. The prince who married her, buried her. This simple page will tell the next generation what my friends and I were feeling. Scrapbooks can beam light into the murky past, clarifying the significance of worldly events.

Goodbye, England's Rose

Princess Diana 1961-1997

A group of us had gone out to celebrate Marianna's birthday. As we walked into her apartment, her roommate told us that Diana had died. We were shocked. She seemed finally to have made a life for herself. The thought of her motherless sons hit us very hard. J. Slan

Possible topics and titles for pages about your times include:

❏ A Decade in Review—what do you remember, what was significant/historic?

✎ _____

❏ History in the Making—what happened and what were people saying?

✎ _____

❏ V.I.P.s —who did you meet, how did you meet and what were they like?

✎ _____

❏ The Day the Music Died—what famous person died whose life had significance to you?

✎ _____

❏ I Remember When—what historic happening occurred?

✎ _____

❏ We Were There—when this amazing situation happened

✎ _____

❏ The Year You Were Born—headlines, photos and stories in review

✎ _____

❏ Natural Events—storms, weather patterns, other natural occurrences

✎ _____

❏ The High Cost of Living—bills, receipts and statements from a particular year (especially what was the cost of a significant event like buying a car or having a baby)

✎ _____

❏ Politics, As Usual—who ran for office, what scandals occurred, what were the issues

✎ _____

❏ We Laughed Out Loud—use comics and funny stories to illustrate what made you smile that was timely

✎ _____

❏ New Year's Eve—What are your traditions? What resolutions did you make?

✎ _____

❏ The Year in Review—reminisce about the year's highs and lows

✎ _____

❏ Counting Our Blessings—a family's "State of the Union" address, how are you doing?

✎ _____

❏ Holiday Newsletter—a roundup of the past year's events

✎ _____

❏ Heroes—who were we cheering for? Why?

✎ _____

❏ Entertainment—what did we do for fun? What movies did we watch? Plays or theater we attended? Musical events? Books that we read?

✎ _____

"Patterns of the past echo in the present and resound through the future."
—Dhyani Ywahoo

"You can train yourself to be mindful by cultivating awareness of where your mind is and then making a choice about where you want it to be."
—Joan Borysenko

*Figure 2-4—***Mark McGwire***. Many stories have new meaning when seen through a child's eyes. My son, Michael, journaled how he felt to see McGwire's 61ˢᵗ home run. I saved the scrap of notebook paper and built a page of memories.*

3. Yourself

We all need to matter, to be heard, to be noticed. Stand by the edge of the ocean and you will see the tide rise and fall. If you look carefully at a pier, you may see a line painted on that denotes a certain water depth. We are like that pier. A part of us is immutable, unchanging like that painted line. Another part changes with the tides. Yet, you are you, unique, precious and individual.

Who are you? What do you like? How do you spend your time? What are your favorite clothes, places and meals? Who are your friends? How are you growing and changing as a person? What have you learned? What are you working to master? If we neglect to share who we are, we cheat our families and our ancestors out of knowing us. Without fanfare, we shape the world we live in. Certainly, we shape our families' lives and our children's directions.

Don't neglect yourself as a scrapbook subject. Hand the camera to others from time to time so that your picture appears in the scrapbook, too. Chronicle who you are and your singular journey. Leave your family a legacy of yourself and your love for them. You might wish to chronicle your career, your spiritual growth, your work as a volunteer, your role of mother, sister, friend, child or spouse.

Your scrapbook/journal can be private or public, but it should fill a need in your life to measure your personal progress.

> "You always have another chance to hit 50, but you'll never have a chance to have your first child again."
>
> **—Mark McGwire**
>
> Explaining to the press why going into the last day of the 1987 baseball season he gave up the chance to become the 11ᵗʰ man in baseball history to hit 50 home runs in a season to be with his very pregnant wife.

Possible topics and titles to share more about yourself include:

❑ My Favorite Places—where I like to go, places I admire and enjoy

✐ _____

❑ My Favorite People—who I care about and what I like about them

✐ _____

❑ My Work—what I do, paid or unpaid, that contributes to the common good

✐ _____

❑ My Hobbies—how I spend my time, my collections, how I keep fit

✐ _____

❑ Are We Having Fun Yet? Good times and bad ones, too

✐ _____

❑ Disasters—the pratfalls I've taken along the way

✐ _____

❑ Triumphs—what makes me feel good about myself

✐ _____

❑ Milestones—personal achievements

✐ _____

❑ Cherish—what I love, romantic moments

✐ _____

> "Power is the ability to take one's place in whatever discourse is essential to action and the right to have one's part matter."
>
> **—Carolyn G. Heilbrun**

Figure 2-5—**House in Champaign**. When we lived in Champaign, this house was on my way to a friend's place. I knew I would miss it when we moved to St. Louis. With this page, I can enjoy the view all over again. The lattice was made with strips of white paper, taped at intervals to the wrong side of the paper, flipped over and woven together.

❏ My Roles—my relationships: mother, sister, daughter, friend, etc.

✐ _____

❏ If At First You Don't Succeed—attempts I'm making to learn new skills

✐ _____

❏ Silly Stuff—hey, I can laugh at myself (grrrr)

✐ _____

❏ Gussied Up and Looking Good—me at my best

✐ _____

❏ Possessions—what do I own that I value and why?

✐ _____

❏ Growing Up—what happened while I was growing up and how I coped

✐ _____

❏ My Family—how my family that has affected me and my relationships

✐ _____

❏ My Rites of Passage—high points in my life

✐ _____

❏ Favorite Sayings—favorite quotations and illustrations

✐ _____

As you can see, these themes are eclectic. Of course, you'll want to preserve the typical "Kodak" moments of life. But these themes are offered as a chance to go beyond the stereotypical life happenings and reveal more of who you are.

*Figure 2-6—**Acorn Theory**. We often wind up with pictures of everyone in the family but the scrapbooker. This page shares my career journey as a writer. My grandmother's letter praises the writing I was doing back in grade school. The list of published works connects today's accomplishments to yesterday's dreams.*

The Good, the Bad and the Unspeakably Sad

Even if life were a rose garden, we'd still have to contend with the thorns. While you may want a book that's sunshine and light, you don't want to sugarcoat the rough patches. It might be tough to share photos of your chemotherapy treatment over dinner, but by gosh, you lived through it and you don't want to downplay your courage. What to do?

❏ Create a scrapbook or two or three for public consumption and other scrapbooks and journals for your heart and soul.

❏ Use envelopes, pockets and memento bags to hold more descriptive information that the casual observer won't access.

❏ Slip a more detailed piece of information or photo between two scrapbook pages. Note on the outside pages that an extra page is inside.

❏ Fold the written material so that it is hidden to the casual viewer.

❏ Keep a journal of your innermost thoughts and scrapbook only what you are willing to share.

❏ Create a scrapbook just for specific members of the family, writing with one or two people in mind.

Make a Choice, Have a Purpose

Decide early on what your scrapbook will be. Is this a "brag book" filled with scrubbed, smiling faces? Or is this a testament to your life? Are you hooked on perfection? Or are you comfortable with reality?

With courage, you can create a book filled with your life—funny, beautiful and wonderfully imperfect. You can chronicle the humor that accompanies our quest to "have it all." Or you can present an image of poised perfection. You are the scriptwriter, the director and the person who makes the final decisions.

> "There is a saying that you bury your parents in the cemetery, but children are buried in your heart."
>
> **—Kee Kim**

*Figure 2-7—***Memories of Josh**. My nephew, Joshua David Newell, was killed one month before his fifth birthday. These memorial pages celebrate his brief, but significant, life by keeping his memory alive.

"Where do the rainbows go?"

Joshua David Newell
(August 18, 1976 — July 6, 1981)

"It is only with the heart that one can see rightly; what is essential is invisible to the eye."
The Little Prince
Saint-Exupéry

~Memories of Josh~

The day Josh was born, I brought donuts in to work and announced, "I'm an aunt!" I was so excited.

I used to jiggle him and chant, "Oh, by gosh, my name is Josh." He would giggle.

Josh and his mother Jane were very close. They often took road trips to visit me or Grandma Marge. Once Jane called to say they were delayed and a little voice in the background yelled, "Tell Aunt Jonie I had ba-ba-rhea!"

Josh was a great practical joker. He used to climb up in the cabinets in his house in Griffith and hide. We'd search and call for him. Then, we'd hear a snicker...

Once he climbed over the 6' fence in his backyard and walked to the side of the highway. We were all shook up by that. His diaper was hanging from the top of the fence.

On the day before he died, Josh and I were walking on the beach, and we saw two rainbows. He asked me, "Where do the rainbows go?" And, I told him that they are really always there, but sometimes we can't see them.

Sometimes I think he is always near, but I just can't see him.

Love, aunt Jonie

My scrapbook is most honest and useful when it says, "Yes, here are my life's highlights—but please note, this is also the journey of one meager human being and her family trying to create their space in this world."

Since I don't always have photos that illustrate exactly what I think or feel, I have a wish list of what I'd like to include on my pages. After going through this list, I've found it easier to pinpoint moments that are important to me and to make sure I take photos or find illustrations to use on my pages.

A journal is different from a scrapbook. A journal and a diary both serve as places where one's innermost thoughts are written, and occasionally illustrated. These forms of memorabilia are typically very personal ways to save our thoughts and to keep us in touch with our emotional selves. A daily journal or diary is a good place to look for raw material you will edit and re-write in your scrapbook.

Key Questions for Scrapbookers

Consider these questions to decide what you want to actively pursue for your scrapbook:

❑ Who do I love?

✎ _____

❑ Who has been significant in my life?

✎ _____

❑ What do I like to do?

✎ _____

❑ What do I care about?

✎ _____

❑ How do I spend my time?

✎ _____

❑ What would I miss if it were lost?

✎ _____

❑ What special memories would I like to keep?

✎ _____

❑ What customs or special rituals do I have?

✎ _____

❑ Where does my life begin?

✎ _____

❑ What has happened during my lifetime that was important to me?

✎ _____

❑ How do I make my living?

✎ _____

❑ IIow do I show my faith?

✎ _____

❑ How do I express my gratitude?

✎ _____

"When your most important goals are being met, less important things won't matter so much."
—**Elaine St. James**

❑ What family stories do we tell again and again?

✎ _____

❑ What favorite foods do we have?

✎ _____

❑ What are my favorite places?

✎ _____

❑ What do we do frequently, routinely?

✎ _____

❑ What do we do with our free time?

✎ _____

❑ What hobbies do I have?

✎ _____

❑ What sorts of pets do I have or animals I enjoy?

✎ _____

❑ What cultural events do I attend?

✎ _____

❑ What does my heart good?

✎ _____

❑ What books, sayings, philosophies matter to me?

✎ _____

❑ What makes me laugh?

✎ _____

❑ What makes me cry?

✎ _____

❑ What important people have I met?

✎ _____

❑ Who have I lost?

✎ _____

❑ Who do I turn to when I am blue?

✎ _____

❑ What is unique about me and about my family?

✎ _____

❑ Where do I like to visit?

✎ _____

❑ What music do I enjoy?

✎ _____

❑ What interesting projects has my child done in school?

✎ _____

❑ What sorts of correspondence have I kept and why?

✎ _____

"The best resource against the world's stupidity, meanness and despair is simply telling the truth with all its ambiguity and complexity. We all can make a difference by simply sharing our own stories with real people in real times and places."

—**Mary Pipher**

Consider this list as an ongoing set of possibilities for scrapbooking. But, don't wait until you finish answering all these questions to start scrapbooking. Instead, keep a copy of the questions with your scrapbook supplies and refer to the questions when you need inspiration.

Planning Your Albums

Once you've decided what you want to scrapbook, you can begin to plan your pages. You may want to consider how best to display your story-telling pages:

❑ One album or several? You could copy pages to make a book for each member of the family or each side of the family. If you plan to duplicate your album, the $8\frac{1}{2}$" x 11" page will be much easier to photocopy than the larger 12" x 12" page.

❑ Special theme? Pages can be created to make wedding albums, baby albums, holiday albums, teen albums, career albums, anniversary albums, vacation albums, family history albums, school days albums and on and on. If you are planning a special theme, you may want to keep similar colors or papers on all the pages. Or you may wish to create a more comprehensive album with several themes inside.

❑ What size will your album be? How many pages will you need? Take into account the number of photos you have, the space the album may be stored in and portability issues. (Smaller albums are easier to carry and store and quicker to complete.)

❑ How changeable will your album be? Will you want to rearrange the pages at another date? Some albums come pre-bound. You cannot remove and change around the pages in them. Others offer pages that interchange with the snap of a ring binder. Still others use straps, making pages more difficult to remove, but not impossible. Do you see this album as being finished once and for all at a future time? Or do you envision an album that might change and grow?

❑ What memorabilia would you like to display? Molded memorabilia saving pages take up a lot of room. If you value old family correspondence, you may wish to put pages inside a top-loading archivally safe sleeve protector. The page protector is open at the top, but enclosed on three sides so that you can save memorabilia in the sleeve along with your page. Check to see that you can find page protectors of the right size for your album.

"My bookshelves house volumes of photo albums... For me, the richest part of these years doesn't show up in photographs, so I collect my boys' stories as well. I listen very carefully, and then I write them down word for word. Sometimes, when a narration accompanies a piece of art, I include it as a caption and then I frame it and hang it on the wall."

—Karen Levine

3 Telling Stories With Images

The weather stations tracking hurricane Andrew announced the storm was headed for the Florida coast. My family packed their belongings and filled milk jugs with tap water. My brother-in-law Mike nailed plywood over all the windows as the helicopters flew overhead and ordered evacuation. With a car full of clothes and pets, my sisters, brother-in-law, mother and two nieces joined the long parade of cars heading inland.

"Funny," said my sister Margaret later, "You think you know what you would take. When it gets right down to packing, you see what's really irreplaceable in life—our photos. The only thing we couldn't replace is our history. We can buy new everything else, but I can never replace our family photos."

Preserving Family Photos and Memorabilia

Since our photos mean so much, taking simple steps to preserve them makes sense. Strangely enough, the places we typically store family photos are the places most likely to ruin their images. Check through this list of photo and memorabilia do's and don'ts to see if your memories are at risk.

Do: Archival photo albums
Don't: Magnetic photo albums

Do: Out of direct sun
Don't: Direct sunlight

Do: Dry, cool place
Don't: Damp, hot place (basement or attic)

Photocopy black and white photos on a color photocopier because they aren't really black and white but usually contain shades of brown, tan, gray, black and white.

Once you have your photos out of the old albums, store the photos in inert plastic sleeves by topic or theme. You can then put these sleeves into a larger non-archival box such as the lidded boxes reams of paper come in.

Do: Archival photo sleeves
Don't: PVC plastic sleeves

Do: Acid-free tissue paper
Don't: Regular tissue paper

Do: Archival laminating film
Don't: Standard lamination

Do: Archival negative sleeves
Don't: Plastic negative sleeves

Do: Archival photo storage boxes
Don't: Shoe boxes

Do: Store vertically
Don't: Store horizontally

Remember, if the product doesn't say "archival quality," you are taking a risk. If you are unsure, ask the manufacturer's customer service representative. If the storage product is paper, you can use a pH test pen to see whether it is acid-free (safe for storage) or high-acid (not safe for storage). Also be aware that acid migrates. Therefore, you won't want to store old newspapers, which are full of acid, side by side with photos. Instead, put all your photos together in an archival storage box and slip the newspapers into an archival, inert plastic page sleeve so the acid won't migrate.

Working with Old Photo Albums

Ironically, an old "magnetic" photo album designed to safeguard your pictures is actually your photos' most dangerous home. You'll want to remove these photos pronto, but that's not an easy job.

To get photos out of a "magnetic" album, use a hairdryer to gently warm the page. Blow the warm air over the surface for a few minutes. Shake the dryer from side to side gently so that the full force of the hot air doesn't hit one spot. After a few minutes, test an edge of the plastic sheet or the photo to see if you have loosened the waxy film. Or slide a piece of dental floss or the edge of an index card under the photos to lift them off the page.

If the photos won't come loose, color photocopy the entire page. At least then you'll have a copy of the photo, even if you can't pry the original loose.

To remove photos which have been glued, try using un-du™ or Goo Gone® Sticker Lifter™ on a photo that is NOT irreplaceable. (However, I have never had any photo or embellishment ruined by either product.) Number the photos in a way that corresponds to their old places on the page. Or first make a black and white copy of each page. That way you can refer to any journaling in the old album.

Figure 3-1—**Post-It™ notes** help you quickly identify different groups of photos. This way, you can divide your pictures by date, person or theme. You might even get fancy and use different colored notes for each different category.

The optimal way to take apart an old album would be to color photocopy each page first and then try to remove old photos.

If your old photos have been held in place by photo corners, you're in luck. Gently slip the photo out of the corners. Don't neglect to find a way to key the photos to any writing on the original pages so you don't lose those stories.

If you can't get the photos off the paper pages, cut the photos out of the page. You can place a mat over the photo like a frame to avoid sticking more paper onto the photo's backside. Or you can slip the photo into an archival photo frame designed for use in scrapbooks.

Organizing Photos & Memorabilia

Once you've gotten your photos out of the old albums, sift through your memorabilia and family photos and organize the information into piles. An accordion file folder works well for temporarily separating the different groups of photos, but I prefer using photo storage boxes.

Arrange your photos in chronological order and/or by theme. For example, as I worked through my collected pictures, I found photos of my husband and me reading to my son at all different ages of his life. So, I tagged "reading together" as a theme, and then I created a page to celebrate how important reading is to our family.

As you separate photos from other materials, check for dates your photos were developed which might be on the backs of the pictures, on the negatives' envelope or on other memorabilia. Remember to label and date your negatives and store them in archivally safe sleeves or boxes as you separate them from the photos.

Adding Dates to Your Photos

You can add dates to the backs of photos by writing the dates on gummed labels and applying them to the back of the photo. Or you can attach Post-It™ notes with dates and information. The notes then act as tabs to stick up and separate groups of related photos.

Do not use a ballpoint pen or a pencil to add dates to the back of your

Tip!

For ultimate security, store your negatives away from your photo albums at another site such as a safe deposit box. If you plan to keep your negatives at your home, you might even want buy a fire-proof safe.

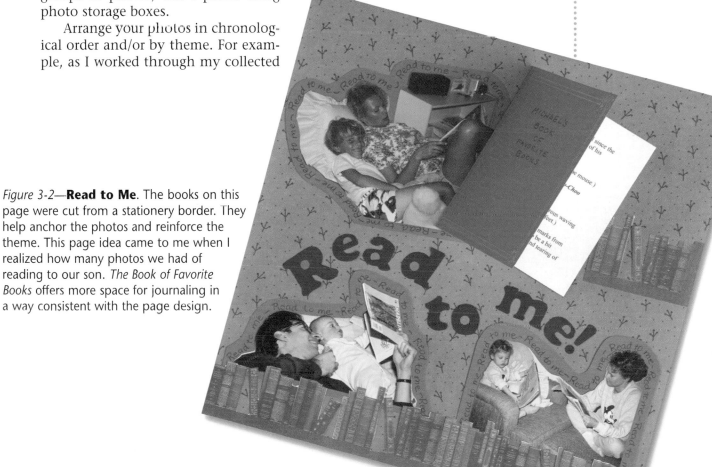

Figure 3-2—**Read to Me**. The books on this page were cut from a stationery border. They help anchor the photos and reinforce the theme. This page idea came to me when I realized how many photos we had of reading to our son. *The Book of Favorite Books* offers more space for journaling in a way consistent with the page design.

Tip!

Scanning your photos onto a CD-ROM offers another route to preservation. Although the lifespan of a scanned photo has yet to be determined, the process looks promising so far.

pictures. You will mar your photo since the pointed writing end will cause an indentation visible from the front of the photo. If you are unsure of a date, write it on the sticker in pencil and add a question mark.

Linking Photos to Information

As you add dates to your photos, you will want to include any particulars about the photo that you can remember, including who is in the picture, what was happening, where the picture was taken and why this photo is important. You may find photos that are not related to a particular event. Excellent! These photos can be used to illustrate anecdotes or to fill theme pages. Formal portraits give you the ultimate creativity option. Use them with any age-appropriate anecdote or memorabilia.

If you don't remember what was happening when a specific photo was taken, don't despair. You are now free to link this photo with a situation that's indelibly imprinted on your mind. (Of course, if your remembered anecdote happened near the time the photo was taken, so much the better.) So, not remembering specifics offers you great flexibility, since we are freed from the impulse to act as a tedium reporter—writing down trivia—and encouraged to set down those memories that are truly meaningful to us and our family.

Taking Photos Today to Tell Stories from Yesterday

In addition to the "old" photos you have, you will want to add new pictures to round out your pages. Combining "old" and "new" images offers the scrapbooker an opportunity to focus on "then" and "now." If you don't have old photos, you might want to take pictures of the current situation and then research old photos to help you tell your story.

*Figure 3-3—***The Sixties**. John Glenn's return to space prompted a discussion at our house about his first voyage. Many images on these pages were pulled from Internet sources, but the White House envelope is from my childhood.

Look for old photos in or on:

1. **Newspaper and magazine archives**. Print out a copy from the microfiche if necessary. Annual review sections of magazines and newspapers often showcase the most impressive photos of the year, so look for them first.

2. **History books**. Make a copy of the pages or buy an old history book from a used book store and cut out what you want.

3. **The Internet**. Print out color or black and white pictures.

4. **Historical sites or museums**. See if their brochures offer historical as well as current views.

Be creative in your search. One scrapbooker photographed a Volkswagen Beetle that was the same year as the car she first owned. Photograph any uniform or item of clothing from the past and use the photo on a page.

You can photocopy any item you can lay down flat. If the item is too cumbersome to photocopy, take several photos of it from various angles. Besides providing an interesting focal point for a page, once you have a great

photograph, you can get rid of the original item. If you are sentimental but tidy, you can enjoy the item via photograph and still clean the clutter out of your closets.

A Crash Course in Photography

Unless you have the training, equipment, experience and eye of a professional photographer, you will probably take more bad photos than good. For any given memory, you may have a hodgepodge image mix of the "good, the bad and the ugly." The pain of it may ease a bit when I share with you this secret: professional photographers take more lousy photos than you or I ever will. But, professionals don't stop with one or two or three shots. They take roll after roll of photos, and therefore, dramatically improve the odds that a few terrific shots will also be in the can. (That's short for in the "canister" of film.)

You can increase your likelihood of getting good shots by trying these tips:

1. **Fill up the viewfinder**. A crusty old photographer retiring from the Decatur, Illinois, *Herald and Review* shared this invaluable tip. "Fill up

> If you have large portraits or memorabilia and nowhere to put them, ask your local pizza place for a couple of their large, clean pizza boxes. Be sure to slip the portraits in archival plastic sleeves and separate the paper memorabilia from the photos.

*Figure 3-4—***Edward Manigault**. Uncle Edward's photo of the valiant plant pushing its way through the rock was probably taken on one of his hunting trips. To include his photo, I had to borrow a picture from his son. To my delight, arranging for the loan gave us a chance to reminisce. Scrapbooking reconnects us to our family through the shared joy of belonging.

Tip!

Add specific information to your photos of your children by asking your pediatrician for a copy of your child's medical records and requesting from the schools any records they might have. This research will give you weights, heights and accomplishments to add to your scrapbook.

the viewfinder," he said. "Get in as close as possible for better shots." Stick to the thumbprint rule: The faces of your subjects should never be smaller than a thumbprint. Get in close.

2. **Frame that view**. Use naturally occurring frames around your subject to add interest to your photo. Take a photo from inside the house and let windows or doorways frame the view. Frame an outdoors shot with a tree limb. Experiment with naturally occurring frames for shots that direct the eye to your subject.

3. **Vary your distance**. After you take that "filling the viewfinder shot," try the same shot from two other distances: move one step closer and then step back 10 feet. By trying different distances, you'll increase the variety. You may discover that the photo that is farther away tells a better story than the close up shot or that the

tighter (closer) shot brings more emotion to the photo.

4. **Take lots of shots**. If you look at the work of professional photographers, you'll see that for each one great shot they shot 20 or 30 pieces of garbage. Shoot more than you need and then be picky with the final products.

5. **The better the camera, the better the photos**. You get what you pay for when buying a camera. Save up for a really, really good camera and you'll see the difference in your finished photos. Buy your camera from a reputable local dealer who will help you learn to use it to your best advantage. Ask your dealer if any classes are offered as part of your purchase price.

6. **Read the manual**. While my husband set up the photo, Tony Bennett stood patiently with his arm around me and an entire PBS television camera crew tried to hurry us along. David pushed and pushed and pushed the button, but nothing happened. Finally, the professional photographer for the Sheldon stepped in to snap the shot. On the ride home, the camera flashed from the back seat. The gizmo was set for time-delay.

Figure 3-5—**Camera Shy**. It's not easy being a shutterbug in this family. SOME folks aren't very cooperative about having their picture taken. Let the humor in your life shine through your scrapbook pages.

Know thy camera. If you can't take a class, go to a camera shop when it's not busy and ask for a quick tour of your instrument.

7. **Snap sequence shots**. By taking one quick shot after another, you capture a sequence of events. Arranged one right after another, these photos give your pages a sense of action.

8. **Capture reaction shots**. Be ready to grab that reaction shot! Anticipate the motion and you will be rewarded with great action and reaction shots. Being prepared gives you the best photos of kids drinking out of garden hoses, people opening gifts, ballplayers hitting homeruns and winners accepting awards.

9. **Watch for backlighting**. Avoid photos with the sun or light source behind the subject The light will overwhelm the subject.

10. **Get flashy in the snow**. Seems counterintuitive, but when taking photos on a snowy day, use your flash. The light from the camera offsets the light of the snow.

11. **Photograph people, purchase panoramas**. Unless you are a real whiz with the camera, consider buying postcards for panoramic shots or landscapes. People make the photos interesting and give a sense of size to the photo. Even if you take a great people-less shot, postcards often have interesting information tidbits you can use while journaling.

12. **Photograph the location**. Call them "locator shots," and point your camera at the sign, mile marker or plaque. Blown up, the locator photo may make an interesting headline for your page. One woman wrote the name of the beach she was visiting in the sand and photographed that. Others have posed by billboards. I've even taken pictures of signs so I could later use that information in my journaling. Best of all, locator shots help oodles when you take lots of pictures on vacation. You'll be better able to identify where you were if you can read the sign.

"Film is cheap, but the moment will never come again."
—**Schley Cox**
photojournalism professor
Ball State University

Tip!

The landscape mode on cameras stops your flash from going off. Since the flash range is only about 15 feet, don't bother to use a flash indoors at sporting events and concerts.

*Figure 3-6—***Tony Bennett**. Thanks to the Sheldon Concert Hall and Ballroom for this wonderful photo. Another lesson learned: Know thy camera! The "frame" for the photo was created by enlarging the Sheldon's logo.

13. **Act naturally**. Often about the time kids realize what a camera is, they start to pose. Posed shots never look as good as naturally occurring photos. You can combat posed shots by holding the camera before your face until the child forgets you are taking photos. With older kids, tell them to ignore the camera. They may not listen, but it's worth a try. (Having two photographers also works well. When the kids don't know who's snapping what, they give up posing.)

14. **Vary the angle**. Try snapping a photo from above, eye-level and below your subject. Get on your knees so you are face to face with a child or a pet. Lie down to capture your garden from the ground-level. A new angle can make a subject more interesting.

15. **Be prepared**. Keep film in a readily accessible spot. Keep extra batteries on hand. Buy disposable cameras when they go on sale and scatter them throughout your home, your vehicles and your tote bags. You never know when the perfect "Kodak moment" will appear.

16. **Ask for a copy**. In every group, an unofficial photographer lurks snapping photos with abandon. Ask the photographer for copies of the shots he/she is taking. Repay the shutterbug with a fresh roll of film. (After all, the processing and film do add up. Saying "Thanks" with more film keeps you on the receiving end the next time good photos come around.)

17. **Make duplicates**. Have doubles printed at the time of your film development. It saves money and time and lets you be creative without worrying about ruining your photo. As an additional plus, you can send those extras to family members, who in return may send their extra photos to you.

*Figure 3-7—***Jupiter, Florida**. I photocopied a favorite t-shirt to make a pattern for this page. Taking a photo of a sign help "locate" your pictures. As a bonus, the reverse side of the sig holds a letter from my mother to my son written as we left Florida for home.

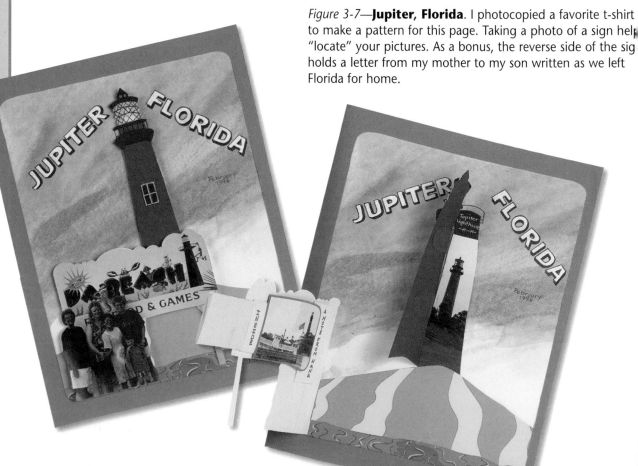

18. **Buy postcards and save brochures**. Not only are they useful for panoramic views and shots you couldn't possibly have gotten, but postcards can be cut into lettering for headlines. Plus, the verbiage on the back of the card will help you with your journaling. Last, but not least, in the case of complete and total photo failure, at least you can prove you were there.

19. **Pick and choose**. You'll save money if your developer allows you to discard photos that don't come out well. While you might pocket less than five cents a photo, over a year of scrapbooking that money can add up. Ask your photo developer about their photo return policy so you are clear about the rules.

Photo-Journaling Your Scrapbook

Writing in scrapbooks has been incorrectly called "photo-journaling." Real photo-journaling is the art of telling stories through photography. A single shot filled with drama can speak volumes. Consider the photo of the fireman holding the child, Bailey, who was killed in the Oklahoma bombing blast. The anguish on the rescuer's face, the drooping tiny anklet, gave mute voice to the tragedy. In other instances, a series of shots will best tell the tale.

You'll be most successful when using photos to illustrate a process, a situation with a beginning, middle and end. Start your shots with preparation, include the actual event and end with the cleanup or concluding activities. Examples of a photo-journaling theme include: a baby's first bath, a walk in the neighborhood with a child, attending obedience school with your dog, moving your household, dad and a child washing the car, preparing a holiday meal, working on a craft project, attending a big event, planting a garden, building a Legos model, making apple pie or participating in a recital.

Photograph every aspect of the theme, using lots of film. If you have a camera that can quickly take one

More and more properties (hotel, motel and resorts) are including a color postcard in the amenities you'll find in your room. Be sure to ask for a copy if you don't find one.

Figure 3-8—**Fish Tales**. Vary the angle at which you take a photo to add interest. Notice how the photo of Michael and me on the right was taken from above us. The fish border is cut from stationery, and the art in the journaling boxes was made with punches.

photo after another, so much the better. For outstanding results, ask your spouse or a friend to join you in shooting photos since two angles are better than one.

By choosing a theme related to daily life, you will give your viewers a sense of "being there." A page where photos dominate allows you to show detail that is otherwise lost. Be sure to get as close to the subject as possible so your photos include tight photos of facial expressions. When your subject is young, your photos reflecting the intensity of a child's interest will be unforgettable.

Here are a few more photo tips to help you get those "oooohhh-aaaahhh" pictures we all love:

❑ When taking a picture of a crowd of people, you'll need to take almost as many pictures as there are people to insure a great photo.

❑ Think twice before you hand your camera over to a stranger so that you can get a photo of everyone in your group. My sister Jane was thrilled about going to a Grateful Dead concert with her new boyfriend, Tony. Jane and Tony flagged down a fellow concertgoer who agreed to take their photo. The concertgoer snapped the picture and ran off into the crowd with their camera.

❑ Create stickers that say, "Property of (Your Name), phone and reward." Slap those on all your cameras and equipment.

❑ Your best bet for camping trips, beach trips, swimming pool visits and water park trips is a disposable camera. You can leave your camera with your things and not worry about it being stolen. Why steal a camera with photos of other people?

❑ Pay particular attention to an activity typical of your child. We often concentrate on holidays and rites of passage and forget the daily "love to do" activities that are so much a part of our kids' personalities. One scrapbooker created an extraordinary page by taking a roll of photos of her son playing in a rain puddle.

> "The photographs, like the documents, have not been well preserved. Because of the blotches and stains, the dust on the microfilms and the crumbling edges of the papers, I seem to hear his voice through a heavy static, coming from far away."
>
> —**Kirsten Bakis**

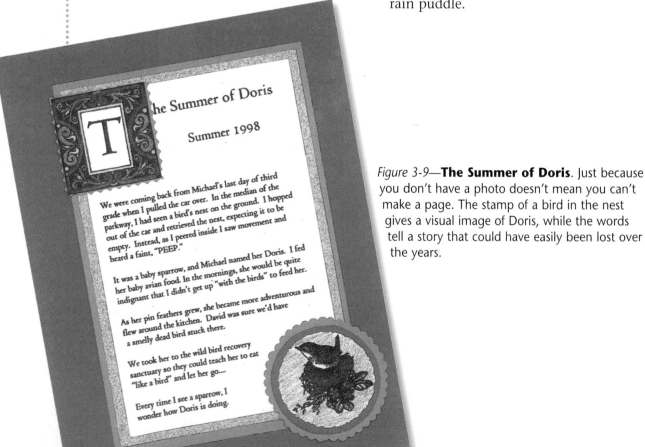

*Figure 3-9—***The Summer of Doris***. Just because you don't have a photo doesn't mean you can't make a page. The stamp of a bird in the nest gives a visual image of Doris, while the words tell a story that could have easily been lost over the years.*

The Missing Photo

You've got the story, anecdote or information but you are missing a way to illustrate your text. Maybe one of these situations sounds familiar:

Scenario One: You took the shot. You take your film in to be developed. Curses. The film was blank, the angle was bad, the person doing the developing messed up or whatever. Your prized moment is gone.

Scenario Two: You've been told your grandfather worked for the railroad. Your mother has many wonderful tales that Granddad told her about life on the Chattanooga Choo-Choo. Although you have lots of pictures of Granddad, none of them show him in his uniform. You have nothing to illustrate your granddad's occupation.

Scenario Three: You and your child are in the car. You hear a shriek and turn to see your child with his lips caught inside a plastic audio cassette case. He flaps his lips and yells bloody murder. Finally, in an act of desperation, you yank the case off his mouth. What a great story. What a waste, because you didn't have your camera nearby! (And even if you did, snapping a shot would NOT have been your first priority.)

As John Lennon said, "Life is what happens while you make other plans." You planned for A, and life gave you B. Your scrapbook sits empty. After all, what use is a great story without a photo?

Well, a great story without a photo is still a great story. Remember, this is a SCRAPbook, not a photo album. You have many options for creating artwork to accompany your anecdotes.

You could use another photo and write about the missing details. You could take a photo after the fact of the involved elements, like the child in the car seat holding the cassette. You could find an embellishment that illustrates a part of the story, such as a sticker of a train or a stamp of a conductor. You could combine postcards and story if you lost your camera while on vacation.

You could make your written memories the centerpiece of your pages, adding embellishments to support your words. The possibilities are endless, so keep those wheels rolling.

"The press clippings are in a scrapbook, and the family can look back at it all with amusement."
—Roy Malone

Explaining in a *St. Louis Post-Dispatch* article what has happened in the year since mother-of-three Michelle Tribout went on strike and climbed into the backyard treehouse.

Figure 3-10—**Gypsy**. When I saw this paper, the memory of Gypsy's bad move immediately popped into my mind. This is another example of why having the story is more important than having a photo.

> "If we had a keen vision and feeling of all ordinary human life, it would be like hearing the grass grow, and the squirrel's heart beat, and we should die of that roar which lies on the other side of silence."
>
> **—George Eliot**

Figure 3-11—**Charmed Life**. On the left page, Mari Pat tells her memories of her mother's charm bracelet, which she "inherited" for her 40th birthday. On the right page, Patricia Varga shares the stories behind each charm, celebrating the love between her and the charm-giver, her husband, Carl. Together, the pages share a story of a couple's steadfast love lasting—and having impact—for more than 50 years.

SAGE PAGE

Forever and Ever: Archival Quality Materials

To safeguard your precious photos, memorabilia and journaling, be careful about the materials you use to create your pages.

Paper—Since paper makes up the largest part of your albums, you want to choose acid-free and lignin-free products. Acid in paper causes paper to turn brittle and yellow. Lignin breaks down into acidic components as time goes on. Look for labeling that gives manufacturers' assurance that the paper products you use are archival quality. When in doubt, use a pH test pen which you'll find at most scrapbook or craft supply stores.

Adhesives—You need to be picky about the adhesives you use for the same reasons you worry about paper products. Ideal adhesives are both durable and as chemically stable as possible. Preservationists also demand adhesives that are reversible so that a photo attached to a page today can be repositioned or removed years from now. Again, read the labels on what you buy. Test liquid adhesives to see if they disappear when dry. Many archival quality adhesives I've tried leave a stain on solid papers but dry invisibly on patterns.

Plastic—Once your page is finished, take appropriate steps to protect your work. Some plastics break down over time to become highly destructive. Look for archival quality page and memorabilia protectors. If the plastic product smells like a new car, don't even bother to check the label. Avoid the product because that smell offers quick confirmation that damaging PVC plastics are involved.

If you have both archival and non-archival page protectors floating around your work space, take a few seconds to mark archival products the minute you open the package.

Embellishments and marking products—Again, look closely at the labels.

If you are unsure about whether or not your products are truly archival, or if you simply want the creative flexibility to use questionable materials, you can protect your photos, memorabilia and journaling in other ways:

❑ Scan materials and store them on a CD. Image storage experts report a high degree of confidence in the reliability of CD storage.

❑ Color photocopy your photographs, memorabilia and journaling and only use color copies in your pages.

❑ Color photocopy the finished pages. You may lose the original, but you will have a good quality copy.

❑ Use original photos only if you have the negatives.

❑ Use acid-free laminating plastic over questionable items. (But do not use this on your precious memorabilia or photos.)

❑ Always use page protectors. This confines the problem to the immediate page so that, in theory, the most you would lose would be one page worth of keepsakes.

How worried should you be? I've heard stories of people whose wedding photos lasted less than 20 years and stories of people pulling 100+ year-old photos in good repair out of the attic. Personally, I take safeguards, but refuse to be scared away from the opportunity to be creative.

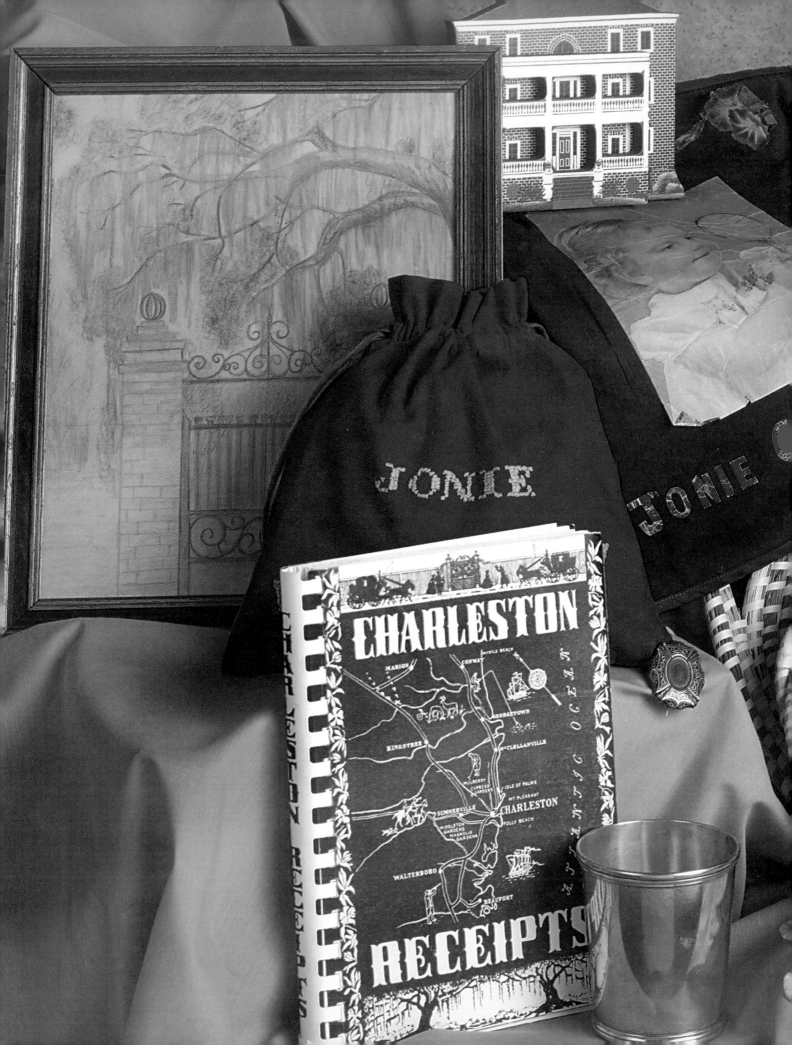

CHARLESTON

MARION   CONWAY   MYRTLE BEACH

GEORGETOWN

KINGSTREE

McCLELLANVILLE

MULBERRY
CYPRESS
GARDENS   ISLE OF PALMS

SUMMERVILLE   MT. PLEASANT

MIDDLETON
GARDENS
MAGNOLIA
GARDENS   CHARLESTON

FOLLY BEACH

WALTERBORO

BEAUFORT

ATLANTIC OCEAN

RECEIPTS

JONIE

JONIE

4 Recovering Family Stories

When my father-in-law, Arnie, sold his home and moved into a retirement center, we inherited a suitcase filled with family photos. One evening not long afterwards, we eagerly cleared the dinner table and opened the suitcase. Inside were photos, postcards, letters. But as we worked our way through the pieces, my husband and I became increasingly perplexed. We were sure the suitcase was filled with priceless family memorabilia, but most of the items were unmarked. We had no way of knowing who was smiling out at us. We couldn't figure out why this postcard was saved or who had written it. We did not know where the photos were taken or who was related to whom.

On our next visit to Arnie, we carried along the suitcase. Unfortunately, he was too confused about what was what. We learned a valuable lesson that day. Keepsakes are wonderful, but without identifying information, much of their meaning is lost.

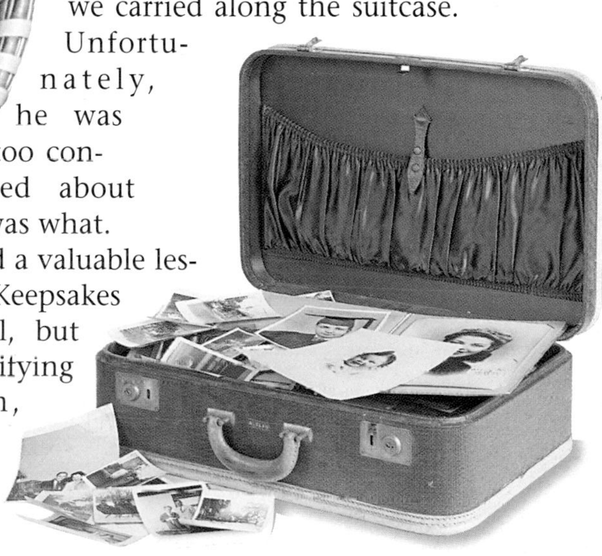

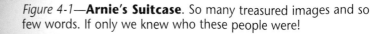

*Figure 4-1—***Arnie's Suitcase**. So many treasured images and so few words. If only we knew who these people were!

Let Photos Guide Your Memories

As you work with your photos, you'll be amazed at the stories that come flooding back to mind. Photos, keepsakes, old songs, dances, fragrances and sounds serve us well as memory trigger devices. That's because people process information in one of three ways.

1. **Auditory learners**. A song or sound from your past will trigger old memories because they are linked in your mind.

2. **Visual learners**. A photo or image will bring back information you've forgotten. If you don't have a photo, find a similar photo in a book or magazine.

3. **Kinesthetic learners**. Touchy-feely people relate to the world by touching, feeling or moving. Holding a keepsake, stroking a piece of fabric or playing hopscotch frees the kinesthetic mind from the current environment.

Give yourself time to live with the photos. Ideas for pages and memories will pop into your mind. Share your photos with the family and discuss them. What memories do the photos generate? Take notes as you share. Often, other family members' contributions will refresh your memory.

If possible, go back and revisit sites shown in the photos. My mother drove up from Florida, and we met in our old hometown, Vincennes, Indiana. We revisited the house I'd grown up in. Her remarks helped me remember more than I would have if I have visited alone.

You can also fill in missing information by doing "around the house" research. For example, if you have a picture of a babysitter, but can't remember the babysitter's name, check an old date book or your check register. Look at old address books and calendars to help date information and help you recall names. An old date book or daily planner will provide more clues.

Although touch and taste are rarely mentioned as a learning style, we know that certain smells evoke memories as do certain tastes. Cooking an old family favorite or smelling a forgotten fragrance connect us to long-lost scenes both delightful and awful. Recent scientific research confirms that information linked with powerful emotion stays in our memories longer than plain, old information alone.

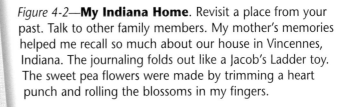

*Figure 4-2—***My Indiana Home**. Revisit a place from your past. Talk to other family members. My mother's memories helped me recall so much about our house in Vincennes, Indiana. The journaling folds out like a Jacob's Ladder toy. The sweet pea flowers were made by trimming a heart punch and rolling the blossoms in my fingers.

Here are ways to evoke and recover memories:

❏ **Tapping your resources**. You can phone institutions, check newspaper files, look up old phone books, go to yearbooks and interview other people who might share memories with you.

❏ **Mind-mapping**. Mind-mapping combines brainstorming and activity to help us get in touch with hidden information and emotions. Start with your photo or with a significant word written in a circle in the middle of a page. Draw spokes out from the center. Write down quickly whatever words come to mind. Don't censor yourself and do write as fast as possible.

❏ **Synergistic brainstorming**. This process works to re-establish linkages. Start with two or three colors of index cards. On one color write names of family members or situations you'd like to recover more stories about. On another color write random words taken from the yellow pages or the newspaper. Shuffle the two groups of cards separately and flip over one card from each pile.

Give yourself a brief chance to view the two words together. Do they bring to mind any forgotten situations? Memories? Conversations? Note ideas that surface. If nothing comes to mind, flip over another set of cards. Keep flipping over cards until your memory chimes in. If needed, create a third set of cards in another color. On

the third set list holidays. Try flipping over three cards at a time.

This is a terrific game to play with the entire family. Remember not to censor your thoughts by labeling the found information as "good" or "bad." Keep moving the cards along quickly for best results.

❏ **Stewing**. Fermentation occurs when our subconscious works on problems long after our conscious mind has given up. Make a note on your calendar to revisit your photos or keepsakes in a couple of days. You might even try a few subconscious memory-jogging techniques such as these:

✔ Look at the photo right before you go to sleep. Talk to your subconscious. Ask it to explore the photo while you snooze. Keep a pen and paper by the bed. When you awaken, look at the photo again and see if more information surfaces.

> "It's important to remember the beauty and lasting value of the written word. It is such a personal and permanent way for human beings to express themselves."
>
> **—Tipper Gore**

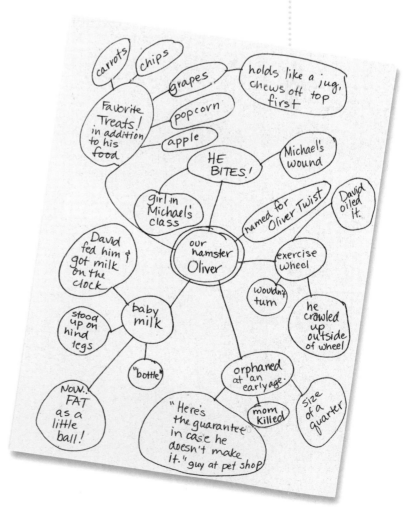

Figure 4-3—**Mind-mapping**. Don't censor yourself! Write as quickly as possible and enjoy the freedom that nonlinear thinking allows you. Some people like to use different colors for different topics. The bigger the paper, the greater coverage you can get of your topic.

✔ Look at your photo before bed and drink a half a glass of water. Instruct your subconscious that upon awakening, you will drink the second half of the water. By drinking the second half, you are physically cueing your memory.

❏ **Interviewing**. Talking with other family members can re-awaken our memory. Share photos with them and ask what they remember.

❏ **Revisiting**. As mentioned before, returning mentally or physically, to the place the photo was taken can bring up a wealth of buried information. If you can't return physically, or if the trip would be too difficult, map out the floor plan of your home or sketch a map of your neighborhood.

❏ **Listening to old music**. A song on the oldies station started a conversation in our car. My husband remembered when he first heard the tune, and I remembered when I did. Then we talked about other songs that were popular and what our lives were like back then. Old music can reach new corners of your memories.

Give yourself time to explore old memories. Often, in our rush to finish scrapbook pages, we write down the most accessible and superficial information. Veneer has its uses, but solid wood stands the test of the ages.

Listening to the Stories of Others

As you interview family members to refresh your memory, take the time to invite them to share their memories. An expert once said, "Children are great observers, but poor interpreters." Your childhood impressions may need to be revised.

As my mother worked on her memoirs, she saw her grandmother's life in a new light. "Grandmere's family home was burned to the ground in the Civil War. After her marriage, the stock market crash and the Depression wiped out her family's savings. She lost a child to crib death. After her husband's death, she was forced to move in with her children. Despite all those losses, she always kept her dignity," said my mother.

Figure 4-4—**Joanna Hasell Ward** was my great-grandmother. She was born on Pawleys Island, South Carolina, July 1859. She was the daughter of Joshua John Ward, the first planter to grow whole grain rice in the United States.

In reviewing her grandmother's life, my mother reconnected with her and saw her strength. "I'd never really thought of all she lost," Mom said.

If possible, tape record your sessions with family members. Years from now, the sound of their voices will be precious to you and your children.

Collecting Commentary

Our perspective on others depends on our relationships and roles. To round out your scrapbook efforts, ask others to contribute their memories about both the living and the dead. Their insight may surprise you.

Instead of letters of condolence, perhaps we should send letters of commemoration when a death occurs. By sharing a poignant memory with the family of the deceased, we give a precious gift.

Taking this a step further, why wait until someone dies to collect memories? By being proactive, you can solicit input from others right now. Collect the comments of others, and arrange the information with the photos you will be using in your scrapbook. As you plan your pages, plan for the written matter also.

Taking Notes Starting Today

As of this moment, you have a new role. You are your family's scribe. Remember how old-time reporters carried notebooks in their pockets so that they could scribble down interviews? That's a great habit to get into.

Writing is much more overwhelming when you start from scratch. Make your stories flow more easily by jotting down tidbits that remind you of significant and precious moments.

I've found that a 4" by 6" spiral bound notebook that fits inside my purse works well. My notes on the spot aren't complete or even neat because they are jotted down on the go—in the kitchen or in the car. On the outside of the notebook I write the date I started the notes and when I finished that notebook. Inside, I write my name, phone and address. At least once a week, I try to fill in missing information and catch up with my comments.

The notebook serves as a tangible reminder for me to pay attention. In a pinch, I've also written on receipts, envelopes and other scraps of paper and

"The palest ink is better than the worst memory."
—**Anonymous**

Five-year-old Peter stood on the deck looking at the sunset with his mother. "Mom," he said to her, "Look! The angels must be baking cookies."

"He says cute things like that all the time," wailed his mother, "but I haven't written them down. I just get so busy. I'm afraid I'll forget them. Any suggestions?"

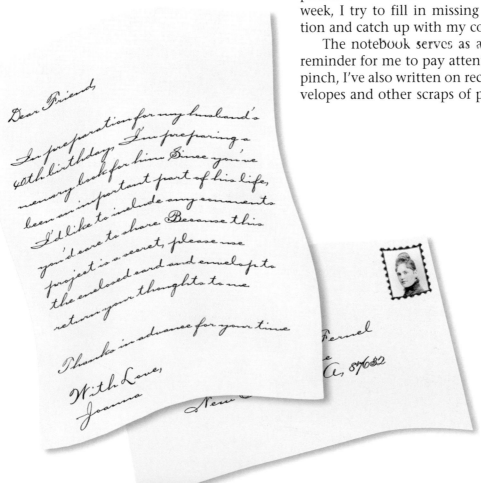

then taped those odd comments to pages inside my notebook.

All you need to capture a story is a couple of minutes. Even 90 seconds can go far, if you use it to jot down a "punch line." Stash several notebooks in places where you spend lots of time. Invest in a handful of small notebooks that will slip into your purse, your glove compartment and your junk drawer. Tuck an ink pen into the spiral binding. Train yourself to open the notebook while you cook or do clothes or wait in line.

Notes bring realism to my writing by preserving key words and phrases. When you begin with a few notes, the entire process of committing ideas to paper goes smoothly.

Keeping Track of Visual Ideas and Art Elements

In addition to the written words, keep visual ideas rolling by using 8 ½" x 11" spiral bound notebook labeled "graphic ideas." Inside, glue illustrations from catalogs, bits of advertisements, paper napkin rings and anything else that catches your eye. Jot down notes to yourself about techniques you want to try or color combinations that might work.

When I worked at a daily newspaper, the artists showed me their filing systems. Under an area labeled "morgue" (their terminology, not mine!), they kept photos, line art, illustrations, fonts and pictures filed by subject. Applying this technique to your scrapbook files, you may have a file marked "Children" that contains greeting cards with children on the front, a photo of kids at play, a line drawing (a drawing without shading) of two children talking and so on. These files help you track and store, as well as stimulate, new ideas.

Finding Information at Reunions

If you have unidentified photos, mail copies of the photos to family members and follow up with a phone call. Can they identify the person in the picture? What can they tell you about that person? If you can find out the approximate years the subject lived, and the location, you may be able to follow up with genealogical research.

Take copies of the information you uncover to family reunions. Distribute your notes. Ask others if they agree or

*Figure 4-5—***Arlene and Manny***. When my mother-in-law, Arlene, died, her brother, Manny, was dumbfounded by the number of people who attended her funeral. Through the comments of other mourners, a well-rounded picture of Arlene Caplin Slan emerged as a proud mother, a happy wife, a woman who helped raise money for the local library, a tireless member of the synagogue, a small business owner, a volunteer and an employee of the local health department.*

Manny shook his head as we stood at the grave side, and he wiped his eyes. "I never really knew her," he said. "She was always my baby sister, and I never really knew about the life she made for herself. I'm sorry that it took her death for me to realize what I lost."

have differing information. Bring along the photos you are working with because the pictures will spark hidden troves of memory. You may wish to have copies of photos made to distribute, in case a family member could jog a memory by hanging on to a picture and reviewing it. (We've learned the hard way never to give away your family photos to a relative who promises to return them. We now have missing photographs in Switzerland because we gave away originals instead of color copies.)

At a family wedding, my husband, David, brought along unidentified family photos. During the reception, those photos generated amazing conversations. David reconnected with the son of an estranged relative. The two cousins shared story after story about their grandfather, Irv. By the time we parted, the two young men had built a strong family bridge over what had been troubled waters. We don't think of photos as peace symbols, but they can be.

Electronic Archiving

You can also share information through e-mail. One of my husband's "long-lost" relatives now contacts us regularly as she completes the family tree. We look forward to her e-mails, and since we both have busy house-

holds, we find answering each other this way very convenient.

Bring along a tape recorder to family gatherings and record what your family says about the people in the photos. With the recorder, you can concentrate fully on what's being said, and as a bonus, you'll have an audio tape of the voices of family members telling their stories. Even though you have a tape, keep a notebook handy during the interview to write down names so that you can check the spellings as you go. These notes will help you as you listen to the tape.

In addition to taking your own notes and keeping an idea file for graphics and visual elements, it will speed your writing along to also start a file that you'll soon fill with material to "borrow" when writing.

> When I have made notes at tapings, I am always astonished at what I heard that had more emphasis to me in person than on tape. By taking notes, I make sure I have captured information whether or not the tape recorder works.

Figure 4-6—**Notebook covers**. Whenever I see a pretty notebook, I buy it. The only caveat is that it must fit in my purse. Usually I clip a ballpoint pen into the wire spiral. Inside the book go notes, lists, quotations, cute remarks from friends' children and my son, observations, poems and titles of books I hope to read and so on.

*Figure 4-7—***Graphic idea notebook***.* A simple spiral-bound notebook holds visual treasures and idea starters in an organized way. The idea for Animal Kingdom came from a picture in a catalog. Months passed between when I tore out the picture and created the page, but the idea waited for me on the pages of my notebook.

*Figure 4-8—***Animal Kingdom***.* You can balance your urge for creativity with your desire to get your albums done by using intricate pages to introduce a theme or section and using simpler pages to display your photos. The first page of Animal Kingdom took planning (finding a photo of a big cat, enlarging it) and time (adding colored pencil to the big cat to make the colors more vivid, peeling off these sticker letters). But the second, simpler page came together very quickly.

SAGE PAGE

Information Collection Form

1. Name of person/s in the photo (please be as clear as possible about who is whom, particularly if there is more than one person in the photo):

   _____

2. Why person/s in the photo are relevant to me/my family/this organization:

   _____

   _____

3. Approximate date of photo: _____

4. Where was photo taken? (Give a geographic location as well as any other information.) _____

   _____

5. Why was photo taken? What was the occasion? _____

   _____

6. What was the mood when the photo was taken?_____

   _____

7. Who was the photographer?_____

8. Please relate any anecdotes pertinent to this photo: _____

   _____

9. What do you remember best about person/s in the photo?_____

   _____

   _____

10. What was a favorite saying or thought of the person/s in the photo?

    _____

    _____

11. What other information could you contribute about this photo, the occasion or the person/s in the photo? _____

    _____

    _____

12. Do you have any related photos or memorabilia you might share with me?

Your name: _____

Address: _____

City: _____ State: _____ Zip: _____

Phone: _____

Fax: _____

e-mail: _____

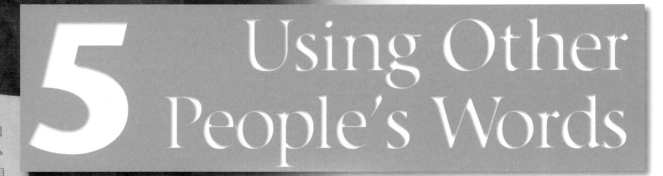

5 Using Other People's Words

Before we go on to writing your family stories, let's stop to look at other people's words. At times, you don't need to do all the writing by yourself. By being open to the possibilities, you'll discover many places to find words that underscore or amplify what you are depicting on your pages. As a bonus, your scrapbook will resound with new depth as your pages appear more like a chorus than a solo.

The best way to start is to set up a file marked "inspiration." Toss in interesting articles, quotations and lines you come across. I now have two inspiration files, each about 3" across. Inside are items such as newspaper clippings, a *Reader's Digest* column, a copied sheet of fables, a page from Dan Rather's memoir and notes I took during a sermon.

You may also want to start a box called a "happy box." Fill it with old greeting cards and other correspondence. Currently in my happy box are the invitation for my niece's baptism, the cover of a magazine, cards, postcards, a bookmark, a quote from Zig Ziglar and much more.

Keep scribbling in a small notebook that will fit in your purse or pocket. Jot down phrases and sayings that "speak to you." Wonderful and memorable lines crop up in books all the time. I rent books on tape frequently, and while running errands, I hear the most marvelous stories—and great lines.

"From all those classic children's books I had copied as a child, I had learned the technique of pulling a key line out of the text and illustrating it."

—**Mary Engelbreit**

Ways to Use What You Find

There are three ways to use others' words:

1. **You can use others' words alone**. If the sentiments expressed by others perfectly suit your needs, borrow what you need and add attribution if necessary for the sake of clarity and fairness.

2. **You can use others' words and add your own spin on the theme**. A few words to explain your involvement or your take on the subject fleshes out the message you are sharing (see Figure 2-5, page 22).

3. **You can edit others' words so they fit your pages and suit your purposes**. By editing other people's words, you can condense material to fit your pages or you can keep intimate sentiments away from the casual viewer (see Figure 2-2, page 18).

53 Sources for Words

Here are 53 suggestions for using other writers' words in your headlines and in your journaling, plus suggestions for where to find material that you can use or tweak for your scrapbook:

1. **Use a poem**. Go to a book of poetry for a poem that illustrates the mood you'd like on your page.

2. **Use a quotation**. Keep a file of inspirational quotations and comments. Even one or two beautifully stated sentiments can make a great impact on your page. Hunt the used book stores for a copy of *Bartlett's Familiar Quotations*, *The Oxford Dictionary of Quotations*, *Master Poems of the English Language* and *The Great Quotations*. Look on the Internet for sites that offer quotations.

3. **Rewrite an old standard**. You can rewrite a hymn, a song or a familiar poem to fit your page and its theme. Use the rhythm already established to help you create your own message.

*Figure 5-1—***Kevin**. I researched two Internet sites to collect my bullet points about the Bichon Frisé breed of dog. To make the "dog biscuit," I outlined one of Kevin's treats and enlarged the outline on my copier. The font for Kevin was my idea, a simple shaping of a standard font that turned the "arms and legs" of the type into dog biscuits. At first glance, this is a white dog, right? Look again. A peach undertone to his fur suggested good colors for this page.

4. Share a list. The dorm sent a suggested list of what your daughter will need to bring to make her room "homey." Put it on the page with the photos of her moving to bring vivid memories alive and to accurately portray what was "hot" at the time.

5. Select a scripture. Bible verses or verses from other religious books contain inspiration and sentiments that have stood the test of time. Your choices reflect your spirituality.

6. Share lines from a child's favorite book. Adding a few lines from *Goodnight Moon* might help remind you in years to come that this small book was a big hit at your house. Or, consider reenacting a favorite book. When we traveled to Paris, we took along a copy of *Madeline* and tried to find the spots Bemelman had illustrated in this classic. Our photos reflect our journey. When I think of Paris, and my son at that age, I remember how much he enjoyed the story of a little girl who "was not afraid of mice."

7. Clip a newspaper article. Let the article be the springboard for your photos. How about capturing the spirit of the "should the toilet paper hang down the back or over the top" debate on the same page as your child in her potty training days. If the article documents a rare occurrence, so much the better (See Figure 5-2, page 55.)

8. Include a notable date in history. The entire city of St. Louis followed Mark McGwire's batting with anticipation as the slugger smashed the Roger Maris record. A page of headlines, photos and our family at the ballpark will help future generations share our excitement (see Figure 2-4, page 21).

9. Clip a cartoon. Include a cartoon that reflects your life or your thoughts. A recent Sunday funny showed a mother caring for her child and noted, "Once in a while you have to take time to stop and smell the baby." What a wonderful sentiment to include on a page for a new addition! Show how the idea in the strip mimics your real life.

You can copy the art of a greeting card on a black and white copier, then cut the art apart to use it as a template. Greeting cards make great visual references and belong in your idea file.

*Figure 5-2—***Cicadas**. They were everywhere! The 13-year and 17-year cicadas emerged from their dormancy at the same time, a quirk that won't be repeated for 200 years. The insect upper left was hand-drawn with colored pencils. The newspaper article was color-copied to pick up the variety of tones within and to protect the page from acid. Although I didn't have a family photo, I was able to re-create the story by using memorabilia.

10. Include a recipe. Better yet, include it and show you and your family making and serving the outcome. Be sure to tell where the recipe came from, and whether you are making it for a special occasion (see Figure 6-8, page 74).

11. Add song lyrics. A favorite song, or one that you kept singing or hearing at the time, would give the page impact. The words of a song might illustrate the mood you are trying to convey. When Tony Bennett sang, "I like the fine way, he plays a Steinway," an idea for a page popped into my head and wouldn't go away. "I'd like to teach the world to sing," could highlight a page with your howling dog.

12. Include directions or instructions. Add the directions to a location and a copy of the map to a picture of where you went. Or include the instruction sheet you labored over while putting together that special Christmas toy or piece of exercise equipment.

13. Borrow advertising copy. Use the verbiage from advertising brochures and pamphlets to fill in information about your photos. If you take the verbiage verbatim, you may wish to add quotation marks around the words to make it clear this is quoted material.

14. Use a magazine page as a starter. A *Family Circle* page titled "Things That Make Me Smile" could easiiy become a theme for a scrapbook page. You can either illustrate what the magazine says or you can use the same theme and write down your personal grin generators.

15. Take a greeting card sentiment. Along with the text, include the art from the front of the card if you wish (see Figure 5-9, page 62).

16. Go to the encyclopedia. What do the experts say about where you visited or what you saw? If you have an encyclopedia online, you can also print out illustrations, maps and photos to use in your pages (see Figure 9-8, page 111).

Figure 5-3—**Steinway.** What do you play for a maestro who has heard it all? Susan played a composition by her mother and delighted Saint Louis Symphony Orchestra Music Director Hans Vonk. The background is an enlarged greeting card sent to my husband and me from his secretary, Pat. The piano was traced from a Steinway template in a book.

17. **Ask for help**. Perhaps the memories of family members and friends will remind you of a thought you'd like to share. Request that he or she write a piece you can include in your scrapbook. Include a copy of the photos you plan to use. When I came across a piece of art my sister Margaret had drawn, I couldn't remember all the particulars of when she drew it. We visited her in Florida where she lives, and I brought along the drawing of the oak leaf. She wrote down her memories, and I contributed mine. The result is a beautiful dialogue page, one of my favorite scrapbook pages (see Figure 5-8, page 61).

18. **Include a thank you note**. Thank you notes written by children add special delight to a page. You get the candor of a child while showing the importance of writing thank you notes (see Figure 5-7, page 60).

19. **Include a program**. Or select a few pages from the program and add copy about what your reaction as needed to fill in the missing details.

20. **Highlight the humor**. So the gas station you passed had a sign that read "elf service" instead of "self-service." Share it with your memories of the trip.

21. **Save the bill**. Bills tell us what we purchased, what it cost and how we paid for the items. They may help you remember an anecdote or interesting tidbit of trivia. (That wild asparagus was nestled in a patch of poison ivy. Your "free veggies" cost a $120 doctor's visit. The bill becomes your poignant punchline.)

22. **Be official**. One family kept copies of the orders the husband received moving them from Army installation to Army installation. On official letterhead, the orders showed the crisp way the service kept their lives exciting.

> "More and more I find the most enchanting quality in people is their humor. Humor, and a sense of honor."
> —**Jessica Lange**

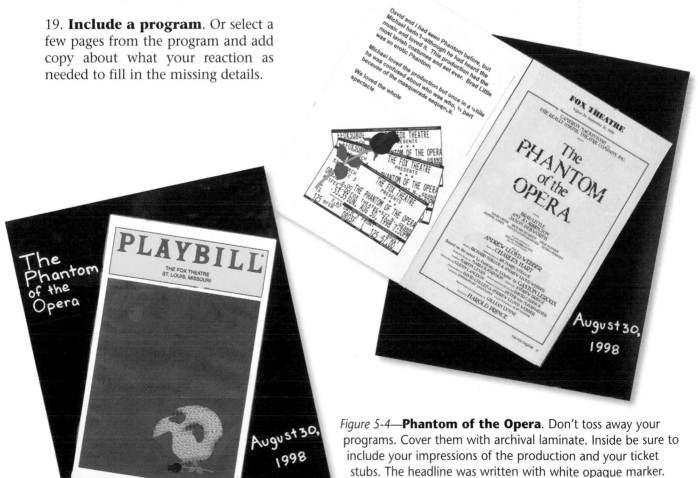

Figure 5-4—**Phantom of the Opera**. Don't toss away your programs. Cover them with archival laminate. Inside be sure to include your impressions of the production and your ticket stubs. The headline was written with white opaque marker. The marker takes a while to dry on glossy paper, so be careful not to smear it.

23. **Take notes**. Listen to and note how a person gives directions for how to do something. Simple directions explain the photos and add to the feeling of "being there." Look at Figure 5-5, below. You get a sense of my son's demanding nature and of his challenge to Lexie to perform on request.

24. **Illustrate your resume**. Instead of a boring page like everyone else has typed up, create a scrapbook page for you that showcases your professional and personal life. Give yourself a visual edge.

25. **Make the alphabet your guide**. Using each letter of the alphabet come up with photos and stickers that illustrate the letter. Don't forget to include words and names that start with the illustrated letter. Use a child's dictionary for word ideas.

26. **Go to the dictionary**. Define a name or a term with photos. This is a great way to create a special page for a child, using his or her name.

27. **Keep the report cards**. A speaker friend's mother has finally stopped lamenting his years of report cards snarling, "He never stops talking," now that the young man is a successful professional speaker. In the future, today's report cards will shed a new light on your child's life.

If you think showing the report might be too personal, create a pocket on the page. Tuck the report into the pocket so that the casual observer won't have access to it (see Figure 6-7, page 73).

28. **Hold on to correspondence**. You might include the friend's handwritten comments on a letter or card with photos of the friend or the occasion. Having written notes from family members gives the next generation another glimpse into who these people were (see Figure 2-6, page 23, and Figure 3-7, page 36).

29. **Save the schedule**. An itinerary or a schedule of events bring the time line and activities into focus. A trip manifest tells where you flew, when and how long the flight was. Airline tickets can be attached, too.

Figure 5-5—**Fun in the Sun**. My nine-year-old son, Michael, made this page. He used die-cuts of the water, sun and corners, as well as a sticker of the headline. Then he dictated the captions to me. We had fun revisiting a good time with his cousin Lexie.

30. **Post the postcard inscriptions**. If you include postcards on your pages, you will attach the side with the inscription on it to the page. Copy the verbiage and position it beneath or beside the postcard.

31. **Heed the warnings**. In one park, a friend was given instructions on avoiding an attack by grizzly bears. The instruction sheet with her photos adds a sense of "being there" to her pages.

32. **Follow the doctor's orders.** Copy the prescription, photograph the bottles and note what ails you. Save the labels and warning from the medicines. Take a picture of the boo-boo and any apparatus prescribed as part of the healing process.

33. **Keep track of the roster**. Who else was involved? What did they do? Why did you meet? Include the roster with a photo of the group or the team.

34. **Select a piece of music**. Choose a piece that has meaning to you. Photocopy the music and use it as a background for your photos.

35. **Create a calendar**. Jot down your activities day by day. Use cute stickers to mark special days. Include a photo taken that month.

36. **Plan for success**. Outline qualities you admire. My colleague Nido Qubein told me during an interview that discerning people had to learn to be kind. Those words guided my actions throughout 1998. I no longer fought the urge to judge, but I changed what I did after I'd made a judgment. His comment taught me a new way to appreciate one of my strong points (the ability to discern what I like and don't like) while adding a new positive side to my personality. I hope to create a scrapbook page featuring the best personal improvement tips I've ever heard.

37. **Spin the positive**. Include a brochure or page from an annual report about the business you are in. Add photos of where you work and your co-workers. Amplify the positives noted in the report.

> "I have often thought that the best way to define a man's character would be to seek out the particular mental or moral attitude in which, when it came upon him, he felt himself most deeply and intensely active and alive. At such moments there is a voice inside which speaks and says: 'This is the real me!'"
>
> **—William James**

*Figure 5-6—***Lizard Town A**. Another creation by Michael. I gave him an extra photo, and he did the rest. Then, he dictated the dialogue, and this time, I typed it in on the computer and printed it out in different colors. He used large designing scissors for the mat around the journaling. As you can see, glitz rules with Master Mike.

38. **Revisit a review**. Add the comments of a reviewer about the movie you saw, the play you attended, a book you read, a place you visited or the concert you heard.

39. **Share a floor plan**. Have a copy shop shrink down the floorplan or architect's drawing of your home. Use it on a page with photos of construction. Add pieces of fabric and wallpapers used to give the page texture and color. Or photograph a plan and then enlarge your photo if necessary to show detail.

> "Regret for the things we did can be tempered by time; it is regret for the things we did not do that is inconsolable."
> —**Sidney J. Harris**

40. **Procure a legal document**. Your child's adoption papers, a business license, a building permit and your marriage certificate illustrate the joy of the moment. Add appropriate photos or programs.

41. **Admire children's writing and artwork**. Whether the message was dictated or handwritten by the child, the words from a babe have an innocence we can never recapture. A first painting from a child can make a wonderful background paper for a page. If the art is unwieldy, or the project multidimensional, take pictures of the project and create a gallery page, using mats cut like frames to showcase the artwork and written matter.

42. **Keep a birth announcement**. The who, what, when, where and how long are usually included. Just add a photo and you've got a great page.

43. **Glance over a travel brochure**. You can use the brochure as paper and put the photos on top of it, or you can simply copy the wording. If the photos in the brochure are what you need, make color copies and enlarge them if necessary.

44. **Fill out an application**. Wouldn't it be neat to show your teenager's first job application? Or a child's contest entry? Borrow the wording of the questions and the answers. Use the application form as background paper or shrink it and use it as an art element.

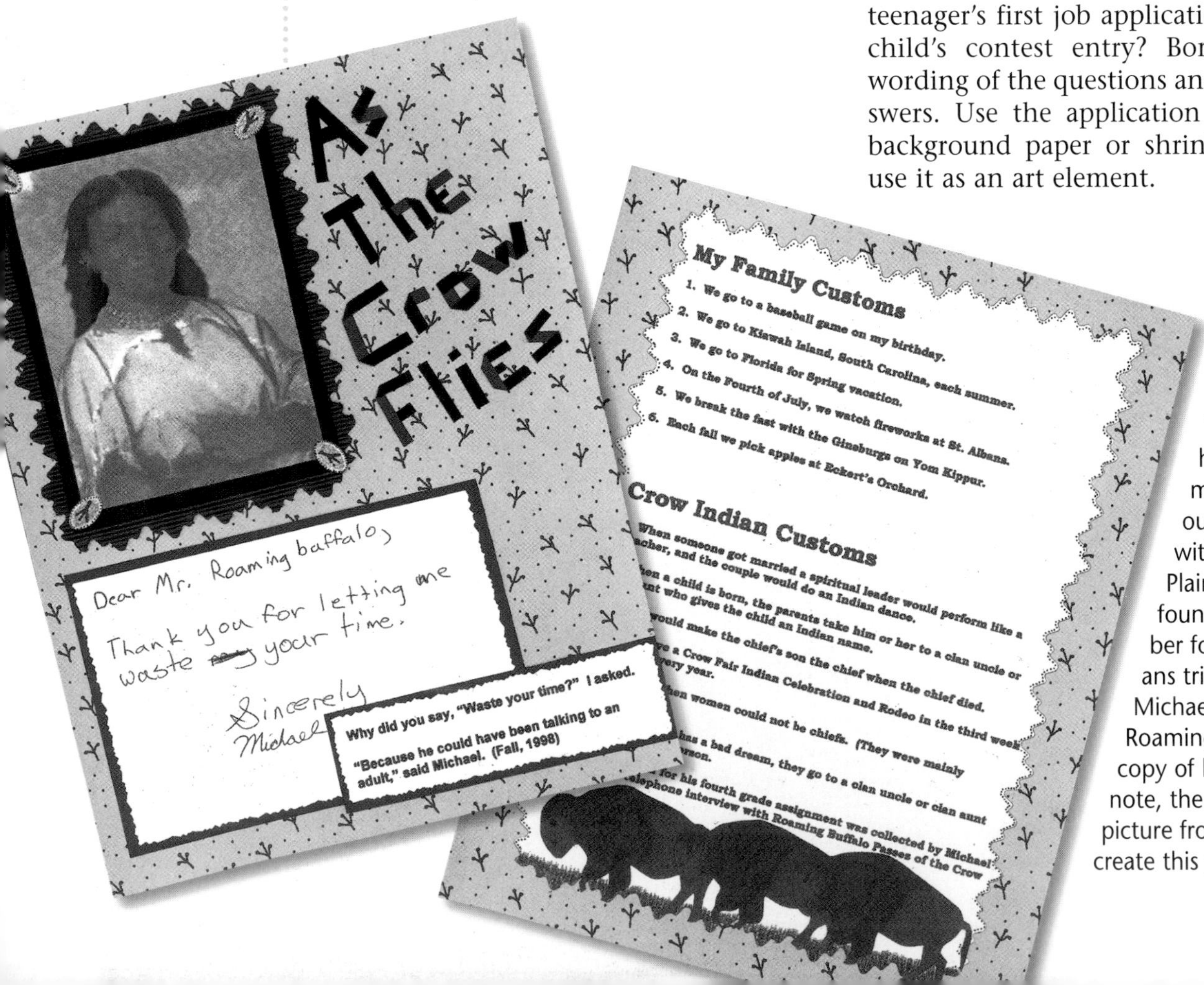

Figure 5-7—**As the Crow Flies**. This started as a homework assignment to contrast our family's customs with the customs of a Plains Indian tribe. We found the phone number for the Crow Indians tribal office, and Michael interviewed Mr. Roaming Buffalo. I kept a copy of his thank you note, the assignment and a picture from the Internet to create this page.

45. Display an advertisement. Ad writers fill the space chock-full with information. You could save an ad for a cultural event you attended, an ad for your job or a "for sale" ad that helped you find your home.

46. Swap business cards. Styles of cards change, and so do the jobs and job descriptions. A business card tells a lot about the industry, the position, the company and the times (see Figure 6-4, page 69). How long ago was it when cards didn't include fax numbers, e-mail addresses and Web sites?

47. Save a family story. Even though you've heard the story of how Grandpa met Grandma a thousand times, your children might forget it. Ask the person in the story to handwrite it out so you have both the written matter and a sample of their handwriting.

48. Twist a title around. "Star Wars" can beget "Chore Wars." Movie titles make great page headlines, with or without a change of words.

49. Clinch it with a cliché.. "Love at First Sight" has been said millions of times, but when I used it to describe how we felt when we saw our son, the phrase seemed new again (see Figure 1-2, page 8).

50. Play with words. As a speaker and author, I'm always trying to come up with new titles for presentations or articles. Playing with familiar phrases, twisting the words, works best. For example, when a woman at one of my sessions told me "I'm too blessed to be depressed," I ran to scribble that down. Now it's the title of one of my books.

51. Keep your ears open. Two men were talking behind me on an airplane. One man was lamenting the good luck of a person he thought undeserving. The second man said, "Well, look at it this-a-way, even a blind hog finds an acorn oncet in a while." What a hoot!

Try a dialogue page with a family member. Take turns writing down thoughts about a photo, a memory or a piece of memorabilia. You'll be amazed at how enjoyable and educational this process is.

*Figure 5-8—***Autumn Memories**. I brought this cherished drawing of an oak leaf by Margaret when I visited her in Florida. She and I wrote down our memories about the drawing, and I edited our thoughts. Margaret was very surprised I had kept this for more than 15 years. Scrapbooking translates the words "I am proud of you" into action as we build pages that underscore our family values.

52. **Read t-shirts, greeting cards, buttons and bumper stickers**. A page that will not be appearing in this book shows my husband struggling to re-seed our dying front lawn. The headline came from a t-shirt: I fought the lawn and the lawn won. (Sorry, but I prize marital harmony too much to share this poignant picture of a man, his lawn and his misery.)

53. **Listen to kids**. Mary Engelbreit was having a bad day when her son hugged her and lectured, "You'll be all right, Mom. All you need is a little piece of quiet." That saying has since been immortalized on her work.

Great titles and journaling quickly involve the reader, illustrate a facet of the story and impact the imagination. Short titles are easiest to read, but long titles will work if they support the image you wish to create. Use your notebook to try a variety of word combinations as you search for one that "speaks to you." Play with combinations by putting words in columns and trying them together in pairs. (Remember how you named your baby? Speaking out loud pairs of first and middle names, then adding your last name?) Go to the dictionary for synonyms or definitions that might give you more words to work with.

The English language consists of about 650,000 words and grows at the rate of 500 words a year. With so much raw material and a bounty of places to borrow from, you don't need to be an ace writer to find the right words for your pages. Just keep trying out phrases and sources until you find the right ones.

*Figure 5-9—***Book of Life**. A Hanukkah greeting card planted the seed for this page. I copied the card in black and white and used it as a pattern. The upper background was sponge-painted. By adding stripes of colored paper to the mats, the visual theme was continued with the journaling. Trimming the edge of the three leaves in gold kept them from blurring into one big leaf.

SAGE PAGE

Little Fingers, Big Messages

How delightful it is to see the world through the eyes of a child. If possible, involve the children in your family in scrapbooking. Here are a few ways to get youngsters started:

1. Purchase a scrapbooking kit so that the child has his/her own paper, templates, stickers and supplies.

2. Save duplicate or unwanted photos for the junior scrapbook brigade.

3. Encourage the child to write down his/her observations or to dictate his/her observations to you.

4. Take your child with you when you buy scrapbooking supplies. (But do be respectful of the store, the merchandise and other shoppers.)

5. Buy the child an inexpensive or even a disposable camera.

6. If the child is too young to handle the mechanics of scrapbooking, give the child a portion of a project such as putting stickers around a border or punching out shapes.

7. Keep a sturdy envelope for collecting memorabilia for the child's scrapbook.

8. Ask the child, "What would you like for me to scrapbook for you?" You might be surprised at what your child thinks of as important.

> **Tip!**
> Interviewing young children or family friends yields a fresh viewpoint. By preserving their impressions, we show respect for their opinions while capturing a child's version of the world. Once they see their thoughts on paper, the urge to write for themselves will flourish.

Reprinted with permission, of The St. Louis Post-Dispatch. Copyright ·1998

*Figure 5-10—***The Pope Visits St. Louis**. This year with the Pope's visit and Mark McGwire's homeruns, St. Louis was THE place to be. By placing the large fleur-de-lis on a diagonal behind the photos on the right page, the eye is led across the page and the mind·"finishes" the missing part of the emblems. Little Alex's essay adds a child's eye view to the layout.

The important thing
is not to stop questioning.

ALBERT EINSTEIN

6 Conquering Writer's Block

Steve stopped me after our first writing class. Nervously, he waited until everyone else left the room to tell his story. Long ago, a teacher returned his composition paper covered with angry red marks. When most—but not all— the other students had left, the stern English teacher shook her head and clicked her tongue, scolding him with words he could barely hear:

"Remedial...far below your grade level... failing... can't pass... never be able to write... forget it... hopeless...." Twenty years had passed and the memory still bothered him. "You see, of course," he said, "I can't do it! I can't write."

At the next class I asked for a show of hands. Fully a third of the class had been told by an "expert" to take a pass on writing.

When Old Fears Resurface

How about you? Did someone once tell you not to write? Did you get back a sheet of paper blistered with red ink? Do people laugh at your spelling mistakes? On behalf of every person who has ever taught a writing or composition class, I ask your forgiveness. Taking away your desire to express yourself on paper is a monstrous act.

Writing is a skill. The more you do it, the better you get. Your family doesn't care about your grammar or your spelling. A story with a misspelled word will preserve a memory as well as a story with perfect spelling.

If you enjoy writing, working on your journaling will be easy for you. But, if it's not, take a few moments to ask yourself what holds you back. Once you have the answer, put that situation in its place: the past. From this day on, you have a new writing coach: me! Let's begin by training your subconscious to approach writing with a positive attitude.

Using the Power of Affirmations

You wouldn't allow yourself to be berated by an abusive clerk, waiter or even doctor, would you? Yet, if you listen to what you say to yourself, you might discover that all day long you treat yourself to a stream of putdowns. Hearing those negative comments before you begin any serious venture can create tension, anxiety and an expectation of doom.

As Pamela E. Butler says in her book *Talking to Yourself,* "What we say determines the direction and quality of our lives. Altering your self-talk may be the most single important undertaking you will ever begin." Begin today by talking to yourself in a positive, affirming manner.

Post these affirmations in your scrapbooking area and repeat them before you begin your work:

❏ Finished is better than perfect.

❏ Writing is a natural activity that comes easily to me.

❏ Perfect is the enemy of accomplishment.

❏ I can capture my thoughts on paper.

❏ Today, I will set down my thoughts with confidence.

The common ailment stopping folks from writing is called writer's block, loosely defined as the temporary inability to write. Writer's block comes in five categories.

Block #1: Procrastination Problems

You could write if you ever got down to it. Nike has the right idea when they say, "Just do it." But what do we do instead? We get coffee, check the plants, pick up our phone messages, make a call and check for e-mail. Now, we have to go to the bathroom and get more coffee. Turn on the radio, put stamps on mail and look out the window. One hour later, nothing is written.

The cures:

Rx—**Set a timer**. Sit down and write when it goes

> "If writing blockage results from fear of failure (as we surely believe it does), from expectation of hard judgment (usually on the part of the critic who lives in your own ambitious self!), what's needed is relaxation and the willingness to leap off a cliff—verbally speaking, of course."
>
> —**Kimberley Snow,** *Writing Yourself Home*

Figure 6-1—**Catching Lizards**. This silly little poem came to me, and all I could find to write on was a receipt. Think "capture" when you think about your scrapbook pages. Ideas flit past like butterflies. A piece of paper and a pen are your net. Catch 'em!

off no matter what else needs to be done. In our home, the rule is "If it isn't bleeding or burning, it's worth ignoring." You can get a lot written in tiny scraps of time if you can get over the hurdle of getting started.

Rx—**Create a place to write**. Make sure you have the necessary materials. Better yet, keep notebooks and pens in several places like your kitchen, car and by your bed.

Rx—**Make an appointment with yourself**. Use the answering machine to fend off calls. To qualify for being "on time," you must make it a point of honor to be writing when your appointment begins.

Rx—**Make a pact with a pal**. Promise to call each other at a certain time to remind each partner to get cracking. Promise to share what you have written.

Rx—**Go someplace quiet to write**. The public library has long been known as a sanctuary for students working on term papers because the quiet atmosphere guarantees a great place to write.

Rx—**Leverage the situation**. Make your writing situation as pleasant as possible and offer yourself a reward for getting to work. Tell yourself that if you write for an hour, you can then eat a bag of M&Ms. (Chocolate always works for me!)

By making your writing environment pleasant, you invite the muse to visit. (The muses were goddesses who aided artists in their endeavors.)

Rx—**Try group writing at a crop**. Set a timer or play soothing music. Make a rule that no talking is allowed while you work on your writing. If you wish, share your writing and discuss what you've written. As you discuss what's written, make notes about new information that comes to mind.

Block #2: Frozen Fingers

Cat got your tongue—er, fingers. You are sitting in front of your tablet or computer screen, and nothing is happening. In your mind, a dozen words scuffle about. Your fingers hesitate, hesitate and hesitate again. Mentally, you struggle to get the words right.

If you are really worried about your composition, first write your work using a word processor. Most programs can check for grammar and spelling errors. Or ask a friend to doublecheck your work. Whatever you do, don't get so hung up on the minors so that you ignore the majors.

Figure 6-2—**Hand Over the Chocolate**. Okay, because you and I are scrapbooking buddies now, I will share with you my recipe for an M&M casserole: In a round casserole dish spread one layer of plain M&Ms. On top of that layer, spread a layer of peanut M&Ms. On top of that layer, spread a layer of crunchy M&Ms. On top of that layer, spread a layer of almond M&Ms. Mix well. Eat with both hands. (By the way, I made these M&Ms shiny by covering paper with acid-free tape and then punching out the candies.)

Choco-Mania!

I love chocolate! I buy M and Ms in the therapeutic size bag (the big 1 pounder). Chocolate makes me smile.

Once when we were snowed in and our flight to Florida was canceled, I ate the tops off all the Godiva we'd purchased for my family as Christmas gifts.

Photo Winter 1999

HAND *Over the* CHOCOLATE And One Gets Hurt!

I urge you to compose on a computer or at least on a typewriter. Most of us will be nearly 20 times faster on a computer than if we write by hand. With a computer, you can fix spellings, change word placement, play with size and font, add or delete entire phrases and on and on. Even if you later recopy your words in your own handwriting, first compose it on the computer.

The page before you remains blank. In translating thoughts into written words, the process goes awry.

Here are ways to get your fingers flying and your thoughts on paper:

Rx—**Get it down**. Never, ever, ever try to compose in your head. That's why the Egyptians first created paper. Write down what you are struggling with and rewrite it until you have what you want or can live with. Feel free to rip off pieces of paper as you go and wad them up. (This is part of the fun of it for me! I love making a mess on the floor that signals I was "working hard.")

Rx—**Just the facts**. When you are really, really stuck, start listing what you do know. Type in the who, what, when, where, why and how. The act of putting words on the blank page or screen starts the creative process. Move your who-what-when-where-why-and-how to the bottom of the computer screen and start your "real" writing above it. This captures essential information, keystrokes in information and fills the daunting blank page.

Rx—**Warm up your mind again**. To get back into the swing of writing after you've been called away, re-read what you have written. Tinker with the words you already have, then add more.

Rx—**Capture the thoughts**. Creative people don't think linearly. (Women are particularly nonlinear in our thought processes. We are by biology and sociology natural multi-taskers. Our ability to juggle many ideas at once allows us to get dinner on the table, answer the phone, let in the dog, pick up the crying child and fold laundry at the same time.) So keep a notepad nearby when you write and jot down those stray "to-do" thoughts and other ideas that pop up. This cuts down on distractions and often yields new ideas.

Rx—**Turn on the tap and let it flow**. Don't stop to criticize your work or make corrections while your creative juices are flowing. When you're hot, you're hot. Write as fast as you can. You can make corrections later. Don't stymie your creative process.

*Figure 6-3—***A Love for the Sea**. Sorting photos made me realize how we've taught each generation to love the sea. Whelk shells provide a unique mat here for each picture, tying together color and black and white. The journaling includes a quotation from Ballantine's *Tideland Treasure* and a simple who, when and where for each photo.

Block #3: Blank Brain

You're looking at the photo and drawing a blank. All your memories have vanished, but you'd still like to scrapbook this page. How do you call forth ideas of what to write about?

Try one of these idea-generating activities:

Rx—**Mind-mapping**. Select a photo or an incident. Follow the instructions on mind-mapping on page 45. Two keys to success: First, write quickly, capturing the first thoughts that come to mind. Second, force yourself to write down at least four or five thoughts about each photo or topic. By writing down more than one or two, you push your mind to dig into your mental storage locker and you recover better information.

Rx—**Fill a file**. Put a picture or pictures inside and a label on a file folder. As you think of the picture or glance at it during the day, drop in a piece of paper with a relevant word or phrase. Remove your paper notes. Type in what you have to begin your writing process. Key to success: Don't stop to sort too soon. Occasionally, material looks like a tangent, but turns out to be a fantastic idea.

Rx—**Tear up paper**. Tear a full-size sheet of paper into 1" by 1" pieces.

While looking at your photos, as quickly as possible, jot down all the words or phrases that come to mind. Quickly put one idea or word on each paper. Arrange the paper squares in piles by topics. What are you missing? Key to success: The small scraps of paper are not as daunting as index cards. You feel more comfortable scribbling down a word and racing through them.

Rx—**Feel the burning desire**. How do you feel about the scene in the photo? What emotional memories are called up? Why? Pretend this is your only chance to communicate with those you love about this photo. What would you like for them to know? Key: Search your heart, not your head. Pretend this is all you can leave behind. What must be said?

Rx—**Write statements**. Write down every fact you can about what you see. Move systematically through the photo. Add any other ideas that come

When you are too close to the topic, or when your emotions get in the way, postpone writing. Make notes to capture facts. Include information about your current feelings, details and thoughts. Revisit your notes when you have "processed" the situation. By writing notes, you'll guarantee that you have solid, raw material to work with. By waiting, you'll be sure to treat a difficult subject with tact.

*Figure 6-4—**All American Boy**.* These photos of my father helped me generate a list of Daddy's accomplishments. Then I added the business card. A phone call to my grandmother yielded new information. Finally, a note from my mother was filled with more details. Writing does not have to be done all at once. Often a piecemeal approach yields better results than one shot at your target.

After I met Van Cliburn, the legendary pianist, I went for a walk and talked into a tape recorder about what our meeting had been like and what he had said. Because the meeting was so fresh in my mind, I was able to record many details. The tape is labeled, and I can't help but think that someday my grandchildren will enjoy hearing me tell this extraordinary tale in my own voice.

as you list the facts. Then ask questions.

For example: The photo below shows Dia, Peter's new puppy. The facts include her breed and the date of the photo. The 20 questions might have included: Why did we choose her? How much does she weigh? How old was she? What was her first night with us like? How did we choose her name? Key to success: Keep going until you answer 20 questions. The first answers are always superficial. The longer you write, the more you unlock.

Rx—**Talk to a friend**. Pretend you are talking with a friend about the photo. What would you say? You might even record your comments first, and then type them up. Key to success: Talk normally. People often feel self-conscious and get all weird when they try this exercise the first time. Instead, enjoy yourself. The words will flow.

Rx—**Tape a Barbara Walters interview**. Work with a partner on this one. Spread the photos out and interview the photos' owner about what you see. Tape the interview. Play your tape and make notes for use in your scrapbook. Key to success: Take turns being the interviewer. After a while, it gets easier. Especially if you can pretend you are Barbara, Oprah, or Rosie.

Label your interview (your name, date and topic) and punch out the tabs on the top of the audio tape. Use a plastic shoe box or a cassette storage case to keep your interview tapes. The interviewing technique can be done with a partner, or using your imagination, alone.

Rx—**Fill in the blanks**. Use sentence starters to jog your memory. Write quickly whatever comes to mind. You may even wish to ask another family member to also finish the same sentences so you can compare your thoughts.

Key to success: Give at least four or five answers to each fill-in area. By digging past the superficial, you'll find rich memories.

Block #4: Irritation

You can't get it right. You put down a few words, but the story isn't quite jelling. Again, the use of a computer cannot be overemphasized. At least be willing to handwrite several drafts of

Figure 6-5—**Dia Details**. Peter Burmester was kind enough to write down 20 details about his puppy, Dia. That list and a photo worked perfectly on this page. To transfer Peter's handwriting onto the page, I used my light box and traced his letters and words onto the journaling lines. Note how asking for 20 pieces of information brings in-depth details to life.

Storybuilding Questions

Facts

❑ Who is in the photo? _____

_____

❑ Why was this photo taken? _____

_____

❑ When was it taken? _____

_____

❑ What is happening? _____

_____

❑ Where was it taken? _____

_____

❑ What happened immediately before the photo was taken? _____

_____

❑ What happened immediately after the photo was taken? _____

_____

Sensory Details

❑ When I see this photo, I feel: _____

_____

❑ This photo reminds me of: _____

_____

❑ You might not notice this immediately, but this photo shows: _____

_____

❑ The person in this photo is wearing _____ and here's why:

_____

❑ When the photo was taken, the people in it were: _____

_____

Creative Memories consultant Dawn Castillo has seen croppers stop and throw up their hands when it comes to writing in their scrapbooks. Dawn makes it a point to remind people gently to write what is in their hearts. If you search your heart, surely the right words will come.

Tip!

If you are forced to abandon your writing, jot down a word or phrase about what you intended to write next before walking away. Start your next session at this point.

> "Being messy is human. The more people there are in your life, the bigger the mess... No mess, no love, no people."
>
> —**Louise Rafkin**

your copy. Even professional writers rely on rewrites and editors to polish our prose. You, too, will discover that several drafts will add polish to your work.

Try filling in the Storybuilding Questions on the previous page to help you organize your thoughts.

Block #5: Distracting Distractions

While writing this section, I received three phone calls, looked for a missing pet lizard, realized I needed to return a phone call, pushed the dog off my lap, poured some ice water, answered the doorbell and went to the bathroom twice. I probably wasted an hour, but that's not important. What matters is that I kept coming back here to finish my work.

Unless you live at an artists' retreat, distractions will be part of your life. Here are ways to cope with the inconveniences:

Rx—**Take distraction as a matter of course**. Plan for it. Use a distraction list to jot down those ideas that come to mind while you are writing. Let the answering machine pick up your calls. Give the kids a snack and pop in an entertaining video for them.

Rx—**Visualize yourself as a boomerang**. No matter how far the distraction throws you, you must return home to your writing.

Rx—**Create a ritual for writing**. The acts of brushing your teeth, putting on your pajamas, setting your alarm clock and fluffing your pillow put your brain on notice that you are preparing to sleep. By creating a ritual for writing, you link certain warm-up events to your efforts. These rituals help build your concentration because

your entire body has been signaled prior to this mental lane change.

Rx—**Remind yourself that distractions are part of life**. Without them we would have nothing to scrapbook. If you allow yourself to expend energy being upset, you've wasted energy you could use to create.

By the way, the lizard is still missing. If you find a stray green reptile inside this book, could you let me know?

Block #6: Fear of Ruining the Page

Very quickly, the new scrapbooker learns how easily you can ruin a beautiful page with poor journaling. Does this sound familiar? You spent countless hours getting the photos cropped and planning the layout. You begin to write and your hand betrays you. Instead of writing, "I gave Lisa a certificate for a *massage*" you write, "I gave Lisa a certificate for a *message*."

Groan. Could be worse. When scribes make an error while copying the Torah, the first five books of the Bible, it must be destroyed—every last page of it! Admittedly, your scrapbook does not demand such perfection.

Now that you are cheered up, what can you do when you write copy so you don't mess up a great layout?

Rx—**Know that you're in good company**. Many of the scrapbookers I interviewed for this book hesitated when putting words to paper because they were concerned about ruining their pages. Laying out pages and working on the scrapbook tends to feed our nature for social contact. By contrast, writing conjures up visions of solitude.

Rx—**Write in pencil first**. Jayme likes to work on her pages either solo or at crops but puts the finishing touches on her work by writing while watching television. Her great challenge was trying not to "make mistakes and goof up the page."

What helped her was to write out her copy on a separate paper, and then pencil it in on her scrapbooking page, after checking to see if the pencil could be erased. Then she copied over the pencil with the acid-free markers.

Rx—**Journal on a separate sheet**. Then, add the sheet to your page. With a little un-du™ you can remove the separate sheet of paper if you later find a spelling error.

Rx—**Cover it up**. Journal directly on your page but cover your journaling with a separate piece of paper, stickers or other embellishments if you make a mistake. You can even lay a piece of matching paper over a word and glue it down if necessary. The person viewing your album probably won't even notice the correction.

Rx—**Go over your journaling with an opaque marker**. Then, rewrite your journaling on top of the opaque marker. An opaque marker works the way white correction fluid does on a typewriter page. Be sure to let the opaque marker dry completely before writing on top of it.

Rx—**Cut out and switch letters that are scrambled**. If necessary, slip a small matching piece of paper under the switched letters. Use a craft knife to do surgery.

Rx—**Take up the page elements, re-do the page**. Use your un-du™ or Goo Gone® Sticker Lifter™ to detach your photos, embellishments and whatever. You'll waste a sheet of journaling if you do this, but that's very little trouble to fix a page.

Rx—**Lower your standards**. Many, many pages appear in scrapbooking

Tip!

Watch people at crop meetings share their photos. Often, as a new person looks at the pictures, the owner launches into an elaborate explanation of why the pictures were taken, who is shown, and funny or poignant moments that happened concurrently. I often think, "Gee, when this person isn't around to share, these photos will go silent." It is exactly what you would share with a stranger that you should be capturing on your pages.

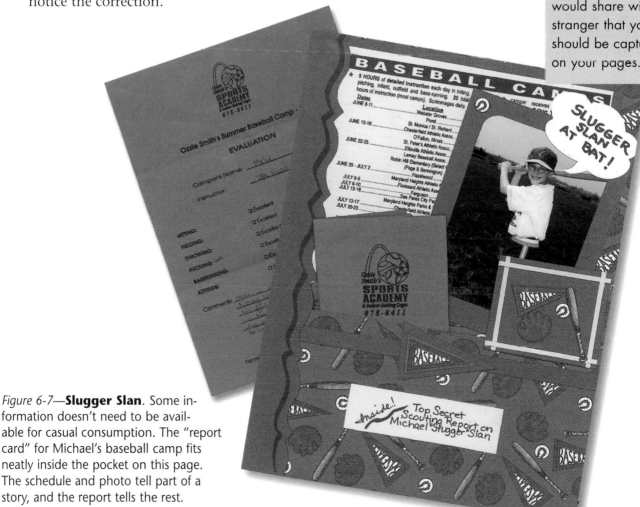

Figure 6-7—**Slugger Slan**. Some information doesn't need to be available for casual consumption. The "report card" for Michael's baseball camp fits neatly inside the pocket on this page. The schedule and photo tell part of a story, and the report tells the rest.

books and magazines with misspellings, crooked writing and imperfect lettering. Perhaps you are focusing too much on perfection and too little on having fun.

Moving from Right to Left Brain

You use the right side of your brain when selecting colors, imagining a page, looking at images and conjuring up emotions. When you start writing or working with words, you use the left side of your brain. In women, the two sides of the brain connect via a highly developed area. In men, this area tends to be more skimpy. Therefore, women find it easier to move from one side of their brain to the other and back again.

However, when you've spent hours working with that creative right side of your brain, picking up a writing instrument and zooming to the left may be troublesome. In fact, the transition may be downright tiring. You can ease your transition by balancing your brain with simple activities.

To go from left brain (writing) to right brain, start by looking at pictures, listening to mood music, coloring with crayons, or comparing different colors of paper.

To go from right brain (page composition) to left brain, organize your work area, take measurements, add a column of numbers, make a list or count letters in a headline.

To improve your ability to go back and forth, take a walk, swinging your arms and trying to move and breathe as rhythmically as possible.

If you notice difficulty in moving from one brain lobe to another, you may even wish to split up your scrapbooking efforts. Have days where you commit to writing, and writing alone. Have days when you work on page layout. Or, split the time you work on your pages, so that you pursue one activity first and then the other, instead of zigzagging back and forth.

*Figure 6-8—***Arlene's Carrot Ring***. My mother-in-law's carrot ring was her culinary showpiece. Although she died 10 years before Michael was born, we honor her life while making the carrot ring today. That's her original, handwritten copy of the recipe in the pocket.

SAGE PAGE
Shop and Crop

When I began working on this book, only one store nearby carried scrapbook supplies. Now, nearly a year later, I can think of six scrapbook specialty stores, five discount stores, and seven camera, paper supply, greeting card, toy, art supply and office supply stores within driving distance that carry scrapbook supplies.

Today, I've extended my quest for scrapbook supplies far beyond my geographic area. When I travel for speaking engagements or vacations, I look up scrapbook stores in the area where I'll be going. When I arrive in an area, I call directory assistance for the names and numbers of local stores with the words *memory*, *scrapbook*, *keepsake* or *treasures* in the title. You'd be amazed at how often my key words turn up scrapbook stores.

Then one night around midnight, I stumbled onto scrapbooking sites on the Internet. Wowie! Using the search words "scrapbooking and pages," I discovered a mother load of suppliers, idea sources, and pages. That night I sat up for nearly two hours downloading paper samples and ordering paper over the Internet.

My point? Scrapbook supplies are all around you. Wherever I go, I look to see if the store has scrapbooking supplies. I trade supplies with my friends and my sister. And, I always ask if the store offers a discount for volume purchases.

If you buy paper when you travel, pack it carefully to avoid folding and crumpling. (In fact, I even go so far as to carry my paper and supplies with me on the plane so there's no chance they won't make the trip home with me. By the way, punches show up on the security x-ray machines at the airport. So if you get stopped, don't panic.)

All this being said, I urge you to support your local scrapbooking specialty store. These are the people with the newest products and information on scrapbooking. Your support of these retailers assures that they will be around for many scrapbooking years to come.

Case Study: Different Strokes for Different Kids

Amy had a wealth of information to share about Allison, her daughter, but less to write about Joshua, her son. While Allison is a socialite in training, Josh is an introspective young man drawn to quieter pursuits. Actually, Amy's terse style when writing around Josh's photos perfectly reflected him. To explain the difference in style, Amy created a joint page for the siblings with a "He Says To-May-To, She Says To-Mah-To" theme, chronicling the differences and similarities between the children.

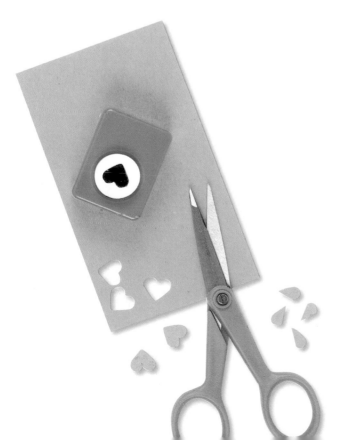

*Goal—***Explain a family ritual or value.**
Example—A yearly visit to a special place, a charitable act or volunteer work.
Images—Any image will enhance the page, but the emphasis will not be on images.
Words—Tell how the ritual evolved or how your family expresses this value. Be sure to share specifics.

*Goal—***Create a record of growth, progress or talents.**
Example—Your child next to a tree you planted, photos as your home is built or results of a piano recital.
Images—The best photos would compare then and now, or show steps along the ways.
Words—Either the photo or documentation could take center stage. Words should indicate the progress made and stress achievements.

*Goal—***Celebrate a life milestone or rite of passage**.
Example—A wedding, a religious ceremony or a graduation.
Images—A photo or a certificate would provide a central image.

Words—Your words tell what this moment means to you. Don't forget to write about the work involved.

*Goal—***Savor your day-to-day life**.
Example—Instructions to the babysitter about bedtimes, a schedule, a to-do list, or a list of groceries and menus for a typical week.
Images—Photos or images would help, but memorabilia or words alone will also work.
Words—Your journaling will give the present a voice in the future. Use lists, notes, receipts, homework, piano pieces, whatever written material you can find that is woven into the daily fabric of your life.

*Goal—***Recall a time in history**.
Example—Momentous events such as a celebrity's visit, man walking on the moon or impeachment.
Images—You may not have a photo you took, but you might include a picture from a magazine or newspaper.
Words—Explain what your family thought, how your friends reacted and what significance you gave the event.

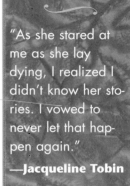

"As she stared at me as she lay dying, I realized I didn't know her stories. I vowed to never let that happen again."
—Jacqueline Tobin

Figure 7-2—
Kristine's Graduation.
These beautiful photos could have been overwhelmed by the bold and colorful paper. But using a wide, solid mat helped draw the primary focus to Kristine and the Sonnett family. Because the photos were taken with a flash, the background around the subjects came out dark. That, too, helped make the people stand out.

Goal—**Capture a memory**.
Example—A cute comment from your child, a funny occurrence, a mess you made or a triumph.
Images—Any image will help evoke a memory, but words may be as powerful or more important than a photo.
Words—In addition to the who, what, when and where, be sure to note the emotions. Tell why this situation was meaningful or unforgettable.

As you can easily see, when the photo or image is dominant, the words take a supportive role. When the words are dominant, the image becomes secondary. Strive not for balance, but for dominance.

Photo Faux Pas After the Fact

What if you would have placed an image in the dominant position, but find yourself with a poor photo. Then what do you do?

Perhaps these common photo troubles sound familiar:

Problem—**Photo is too small**.
Try this—Color copy or scan and enlarge. You can even copy the photo twice and piece it together to make it larger. (See Figure 7-3, below.)
Or this—Duplicate the photo, or duplicate and enlarge the photo.

Problem—**Photo coloring is off**.
Try this—Adjust the color on a color copier or scanner.
Or this—Use a Kodak Image Magic Picture Maker to create a black and white photo-quality copy of your photo. (Look for these machines at your photo specialty store or large discount stores.)

Problem—**Photo is blurry**.
Try this—Emphasize embellishments.
Or this—Create an arresting and interesting headline.

Problem—**Photo has been partially destroyed or defaced**.
Try this—Take it to a professional photo restoration person.
Or this—Emphasize your journaling; use interesting design elements to direct the eyes.

Figure 7-3—**Home for Christmas**. The original photo of the Christmas tree ended about halfway up the tree. I made three color-copy enlargements of the photo. Then, I cut the tree out of one, shaped the greenery to a point, and glued it on top of the tree in the first photo. I cut out ornaments from another color copy and put those on the tree. The "snow" is white felt painted with sparkly fabric paint.

Photo wasn't centered.

Try this—Silhouette crop by cutting out the background.

Or this—Crop to even up the sides.

Parts of the person were cut out of the photo.

Try this—Use embellishments or art. If a head was cropped, add a hat or a crown (see Figure 7-4, page 81).

Or this—Put the photo on the edge of the page as though the cut-off part was purposefully cropped.

Person was in focus, but the background is a blur.

Try this—Silhouette crop the people and add a new background with another photo.

Or this—Silhouette crop the people and use paper or embellishments to make a new background.

Photo is awful.

Try this—Emphasize the headline or memorabilia.

Or this—Use bright paper and emphasize layout, color or embellishments. Consider adding a "formal" shot of your family.

Photo doesn't include you or your family but you were there!

Try this—Take photos of your family dressed appropriately. Include yourselves in a collage of the other folks.

Or this—Use photos of your family and the photos you have. Try to get a similar background.

Figure 7-4—**It's Your Birthday**. The top of Michael's head was lopped off in the original photo so I crowned him with paper and stickers. I also color-copied and enlarged the original, a technique I use a lot, especially to make one photo dominant when I have several photos all of the same size.

Parts of the photo didn't come out at all or parts of the photo reveal stuff you didn't want.

Try this—Cut out the people and adhere them to a new background, such as a postcard or brochure scene.

Or this—Cover the bad parts with borders or embellishments.

For ideas to help you take better photos, see *Chapter 3: Telling Stories with Images*, page 29.

Putting Words and Images Together

When artists want to give a sense of serenity, they show stability and calm. When artists want to arouse emotions, they show motion. Use the same techniques to create pages that either show tranquility or shout with activity.

Yes, you will still use words and visuals to make your point. But the type of journaling, the style of writing and the photos you select will change with your focus. By selecting the tranquil, or formal, versus the active, or infor-

> "Though God plants some lives in fertile soil, He sows the most on rocky ground. For, here, mere struggle to survive soon nurtures strength for greater things. And thus, in His transcendent plans, He makes each man the master of his own destiny."
>
> —**Edward L. Manigault**

mal, nature of your page, you help your story reach an unconscious, emotional level. If you wish to create a layout, or even an album, about your sister's wedding, you will want to create one mood. If you want to chronicle your child's busy middle school years, you'll want another.

Every element on your page will have a mood. Some are formal and some are informal.

COLORS
Formal: Soft with subtle patterns.
Informal: Bright and bold patterns.

LAYOUT
Formal: Balanced, symmetrical.
Informal: Unbalanced, non-symmetrical.

HANDWRITTEN TEXT
Formal: Cursive.
Informal: Printed or child-like script.

WRITING STYLE
Formal: Formal wording.
Informal: Informal wording, using contractions.

TYPOGRAPHY
Formal: Serif type (the type has little feet on the end of the letters).
Informal: Sans-serif type.

COPY OR JOURNALING
Formal: Copy blocks are flush left (aligned to the left) and sometimes also flush right.
Informal: Copy blocks are ragged left, sometimes ragged right and sometimes centered.

HEADLINES
Formal: Centered.
Informal: Uncentered or crooked.

PHOTOGRAPHY
Formal: Formal or posed.
Informal: Person in motion.

CROP SHAPES
Formal: Ovals, rectangles or squares
Informal: Bumped or silhouetted along with fun shapes like stars.

CLOTHING
Formal: Dressy clothes.
Informal: Playful clothes or poses.

EMBELLISHMENTS
Formal: Restrained or classic look.
Informal: Bold or cartoonish look.

BORDERS
Formal: Symmetrical with all elements inside the border
Informal: Elements bleed off the page. (A "bleed" is a printing term for an image that extends off the edge of the paper.) Borders are broken by the elements.

> "After all these years, I've come to understand that the real joys in life are the ordinary ones."
> —**Michael Kahn**

Figure 7-5—**Joseph Quinton**. The photo his parents sent us showed him on a baby blanket. I wanted to increase and flatten the background to make him stand out, so I made a baby quilt with squares of pastel paper. This lettering style by Lindsay Ostrom was perfect for creating the right mood for the headline.

Page Design Supports Your Focus

Now that you've decided what will dominate the page, plan your pages around the words and the photos or images. The average scrapbooker does a great job of planning for the photos, but often gets carried away and adds journaling as an afterthought or doesn't leave space for journaling at all.

Your pages will tell better stories if you work with your journaling as a design element. Ask yourself:

❑ **How much written matter will I need to tell my story?**
Determine whether the photos or the words will be your focal point. In the next chapter, we'll explore different formats for writing. By reviewing these formats, you'll see how to use different lengths and styles to tell your stories.

❑ **Will I handwrite or computer generate my journaling?**
Handwriting generally takes more space than computer writing. Once your writing is in the computer, you can change the type size or style to meet your layout needs.

❑ **How much space will I need to tell this story?**
Determine page size and the space on a page, and then decide if you want only one page, two pages or a panorama page layout. (A panorama page is two adjoining pages which create four page surfaces.)

❑ **Where will I position my journaling?**
Does it need to be right next to the photos? Does the journaling need to appear in a certain sequence in order to make sense?

❑ **What words might I wish to give extra emphasis?**
Choose a flashy typeface and a prominent position for these or mat them with strong colors.

❑ **Is there any written matter that is part of this layout that I don't want the casual viewer to see?**
If so, you might plan for a pocket page or a greeting card layout with a hidden inside surface.

Two facing pages, known as a "two-page spread" (or a "double truck," in newspaper lingo), offer the best layout for telling scrapbook stories. One simple but effective two-page

A photo that shows a person off-balance demands that our minds follow the motion through to its conclusion, thereby evoking a sense of action within us. Our minds work toward resolution of problems and of situations. In the deepest levels of our being, we long to find peace and order.

Figure 7-6—**Baby, Take a Bow**. Mats and photos don't have to be the same shape. In fact, it's more exciting if the two don't match. Here small stars were used as tiles for the letters of the headline, and used again in yet a smaller size to frame the journaling block.

spread layout has one page that emphasizes the visual content and one that emphasizes the journaling.

Because the 8 ½" x 11" pages are rectangular, they force you to create a more interesting page layout. Only pairs of sides are even, which forces you to create an asymmetrical layout. In a square, all sides are even and you can create a totally symmetrical layout. Symmetry is boring because with all its equal parts, the eye can't find a dominant focus.

Create a Thumbnail Sketch or a Mock Page Layout

Graphic professionals know two tricks we scrapbookers can borrow to create cohesive, storytelling pages. Those tricks are called thumbnail sketches and mock page layouts, or mock-ups.

Years ago when I worked for a daily newspaper, we advertising account executives would turn in 30 to 40 ads a day, and as many as 150 ads a week. Often we only had parts of the ad ready. The advertiser wouldn't have

the photo yet, or the copy for the ad had yet to be written, or the price of an item was uncertain. But—the space for the ad had to be reserved often as far as three days in advance of publication. So, instead of the finished product, we would create a thumbnail sketch and later a mock-up of the ad.

A thumbnail sketch, as the name implies, covers a small space which is proportionately the same as the finished page. Thumbnails don't go into detail, but they do sketch out where elements go. You can even denote colors in a thumbnail.

Here's how to create a thumbnail (see Figure 7-8, next page):

❏ Make a proportionate outline of your page (see blank thumbnails on page 86).

❏ Sketch in where your photos will go.

❏ Sketch in where your headline will go.

❏ Sketch in where your journaling goes, drawing lines to illustrate lines of copy.

Figure 7-7—**Brad Takes Off**. The colorful stripes on the tail of Brad's plane are repeated on the mats of the other photos. Inside his Pilot Flight Record are details about Brad's first flight in this restored plane. Add emphasis to your stories by finding clever places to put your journaling. This page shares with the viewer what a flight log looks like, which is much more interesting than journaling alone would have been.

You don't need to sketch elements in the order given. If the headline is your dominant focus, sketch it in first. If the photo or a photos are dominant, give them your first consideration and then move on to the journaling.

Your finished sketch will be very, very rough, but the proportions should be fairly accurate. By doing the sketch before cropping photos, writing the finished journaling and inking in your headline, you retain maximum flexibility. For example, you might discover as you do your thumbnail that all your elements are equal: headline, photo and copy. To tell an effective story, you'll need to resize your elements so that one dominates the page.

Thumbnails drawn of multiple page layouts indicate whether the eye will see the separate pages as part of one story or a jumbled collection.

For the scrapbooker with a frantic life, a thumbnail captures an idea for a page you don't have time to create. While working through the thumbnail, you may discover you want to use a special font, mat or paper to support your design. Using the thumbnail gives you the time to collect all your pieces without losing momentum.

After you have worked with thumbnails for a while, you'll plan pages in your head more effectively.

You'll also find yourself returning to the thumbnail technique as a handy way to work out design challenges.

A mock-up expands the thumbnail so you can work with more definition. Whereas a thumbnail is less than one quarter the size of the final page, a mock-up could the same size as your finished page. The beauty of a mock-up is the opportunity you have to play with design in "real space." You don't have to guess whether a particular lettering style will fit across the top of your page. Instead, use a piece of tissue paper and create a full scale mock-up of the headline; then lay the tissue across the top of your layout.

While I rarely use a full-page mock-up, I regularly use tissue paper to mock-up one particular aspect of the page for size purposes. You can also put a piece of tissue paper over the semi-completed page and sketch in where other elements might go to help you finish your layout. Or you can trace all your elements on tissue paper and move them around, playing with layout arrangements—before you crop a photo and before you mat your journaling.

You can also use mock-ups by making black and white copies of elements in different sizes. So, say you have a picture of a bison that you want to use

Thumbnails and mock-ups are not a new idea. The great artists made "studies," which were sketches or attempts to work out ideas. In fact, with new photographic resources, art curators today can peek under the layers of paint to see an artist's first tentative layers of paint. These partially visible underlayers have a special name: *pentimento*.

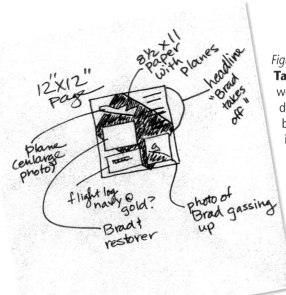

*Figure 7-8—***Thumbnail for Brad Takes Off**. Remember, thumbnails are working sketches not finished art. You don't need to be perfect about size but getting the right proportions is important. I use the margins around the thumbnail for my notes. Two horizontal lines are my shorthand for copy or headlines. If you do a thumbnail with any degree of effort, you'll quickly see if your page will hold together or look disjointed. On this page, the background paper holds everything together.

For 8 ¹/₂" x 11" pages:

For 12" x 12" pages:

Blank thumbnails. Photocopy and use these thumbnail frames to plan your pages.

(Permission granted to make copies of this page for noncommercial purposes.)

across the bottom of a page. The original picture is about 4" by 5". Reduce the bison several times to get a size that will fit on the page. Next, experiment a bit. Could three of these critters go across the bottom border? Duplicate the reduced bison three times and play with how they would look on the bottom of the page. Or you could trace the reduced bison on tissue paper and cut him out three times.

By making mock-up pieces, you've given yourself the freedom to play with your art elements without committing them to your page.

Planning a Theme Album

Looking at pages in a book like this or in a magazine might convince the time-challenged scrapbooker, "I'll never have enough time or patience to do an album."

Finding the right balance between "fancy" pages and simple layouts may seem difficult. We all enjoy being creative. And we all enjoy being done.

You can have the best of both worlds by planning your album or by planning for topical sections within your album.

As an added bonus, when you create an album on only one theme, you don't need to repeat all the essential journaling elements on each page. We already know this is an album about your vacation in Mexico. When you plan for a theme album, adjust your writing accordingly.

Here are common album themes:

- ❏ Childhood
- ❏ Vacation
- ❏ School Days
- ❏ Pets
- ❏ Career
- ❏ Teen Years
- ❏ A Day in the Life
- ❏ Pre-School
- ❏ Our New Baby
- ❏ Grandparents
- ❏ Heritage

Figure 7-9—**McDonald's**. Wouldn't these pages make a great opening spread for a theme album? The title: Life in the Fast (Food) Lane. Many of our best times as a family have been at McDonald's. Be sure to ask the people at the counter for a clean french fry container and you've got the start of a great page. I cut the logo "M" out of a potato, and Michael stamped it on the red background.

Tip!

To make sure you don't adhere your elements upside down on strap-bound album pages, go through all your pages before you lay them out and lightly pencil in an arrow pointing up. Train yourself to search for that arrow before committing pieces to your pages.

- ❑ Learning to (Fly, Skate, Golf, etc.)
- ❑ A Year in Review
- ❑ Our Move
- ❑ Our New House
- ❑ Graduation
- ❑ Wedding
- ❑ Holidays

More unusual themes might work better for you.

- ❑ Theater and Concerts Attended
- ❑ Our Favorites (vacations, restaurants, places, historic sites, cars, pets, etc.)
- ❑ Places We Like to Visit
- ❑ Retirement
- ❑ A Life in Review
- ❑ Memories of (a person, pet, location, etc.)
- ❑ Our Times (events happening during your life)
- ❑ Read to Me (a book of favorite books)
- ❑ My Career

Once you've decided on a theme, decide how many pages you want to be "fancy." Perhaps, you'll open your book with an elaborate page. Or maybe you'd rather include a more complex page every so often. Or you could create an all-encompassing album that uses elaborate pages to change themes or topics within the album.

In any case, coordinate your "plain" pages so that they support the visual and storytelling theme of your elaborate pages. You achieve coordination by using papers of the same or complementary color, the same typefaces, the same mats, the same embellishments or the same basic layouts. By choosing a theme and keeping a constancy of style, you'll be able to put pages together quickly. By adding in those special, elaborate pages, you'll challenge your skills and keep the reader interested.

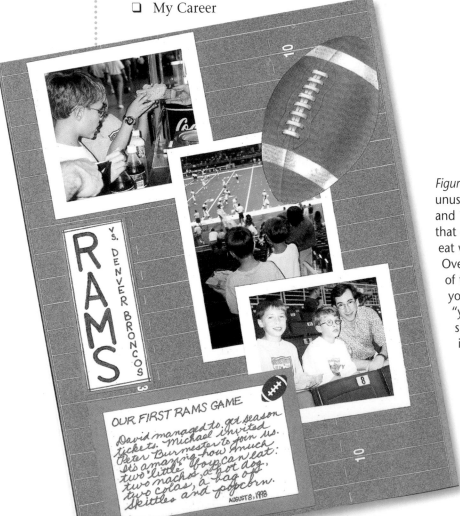

*Figure 7-10—**Rams**. A simple page with an unusual focus: The eating habits of nine- and 10-year-old boys. The Rams didn't win that day, but watching Michael and Peter eat was worth the price of admission! Overlapping your design elements is one of the best ways to direct the eyes across your page. Overlapping also covers up "yucky" parts of your photos, like the signage on the railing behind the boys in the middle shot.

Stop Before You Touch That Glue!

At this stage, you might not have all your elements completed. You may still need to polish your writing, your photos may need to be enlarged or cropped, or you may have to choose your paper. Don't adhere any page elements until you have finalized all your pieces.

More than once, I've discovered that by going back and recropping a photo, my layout will look better. At least twice, I've underestimated the amount of paper I needed. I can't even begin to count the times my headline didn't fit in the space I'd saved for it.

By delaying your paste up until last, you'll save yourself great effort, frustration and heartache. In the haste to "slap down" photos, you cause yourself all sorts of problems, including putting on elements upside down, a situation so common for scrapbookers working with a 12" x 12" strapbound page that it has occurred at least once at every crop I've ever attended.

Once you have your journaling perfected and your photos and your memorabilia collected, you can move ahead to *Chapter 10: Assembling Your Pages*, page 113. Otherwise, let the next two chapters assist you in polishing your story.

> "Inside myself is a place where I live all alone, and that is where I renew my springs that never dry up."
>
> **—Pearl S. Buck**

Figure 7-11—**Apple Picking**. Don't overlook shots like this one of Michael covered by the apple tree. Unusual photos often tell better stories than ordinary poses. And that photo of the grimace isn't pretty, is it? But it's a perfect "storytelling" photo, nonetheless. The large apples were cut from one sheet of paper and arranged in "peek-a-boo" fashion around the other design elements.

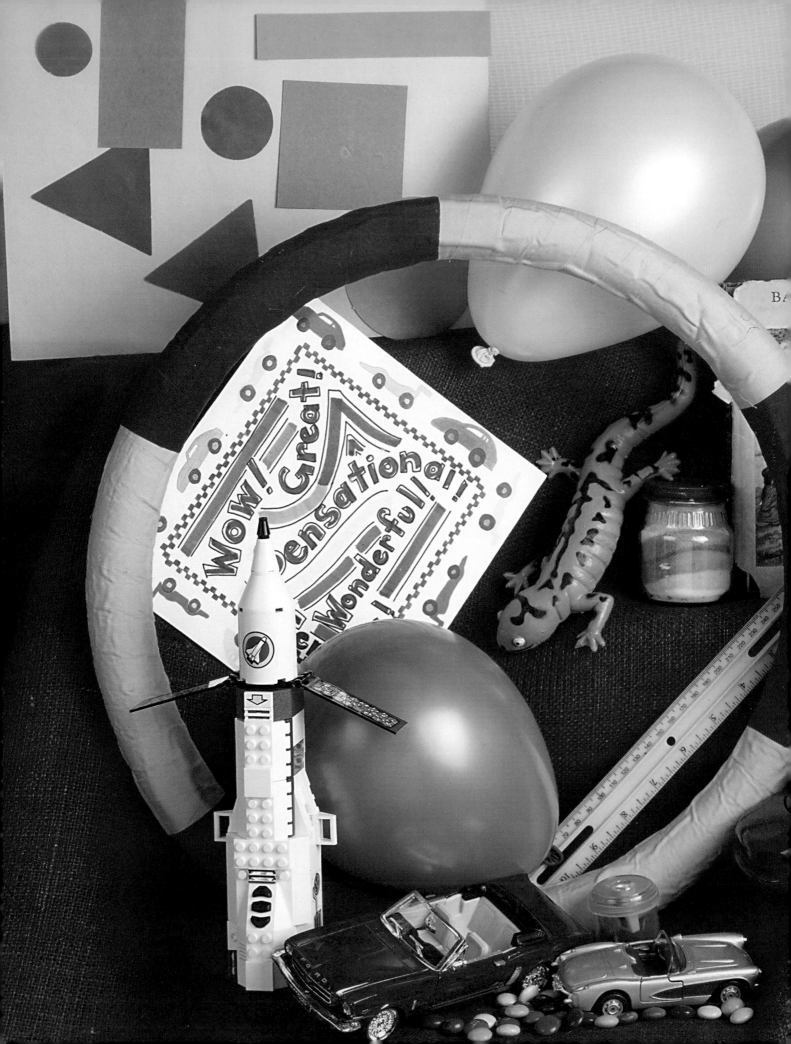

8 Formatting Your Stories

In the last chapter, we worked together to help you plan pages to enhance their story-telling impact. In this chapter, you'll learn different formats for your writing.

Turning Information into Stories

Naming the different journaling formats gives us a working handle, or language, to use while discussing these formats and lets you see the choices you have.

While I'm going to borrow terms from journalism, the finished writing in a scrapbook won't look or read like a news-paper. Not only does it have a different size and number of pages, it also has a smaller audience and a limited cast of characters. Your goals in scrapbooking will cause you to care more about certain elements of your journaling, such as emotions or memories, and less about others.

For example, if the photos were taken in the fall of 1998, that's close enough. You don't need an exact date unless you are called to testify in court. Finally, the use of other visual aids—paper, color, photos, memorabilia, embellishments—means you can work with a limited number of written words and still craft an effective story.

Note, too, that your scrapbook writing won't be like the kind of writing you'd do in a diary or journal. Your journal or diary are primarily written for you; a scrapbook will be handed on.

Scrapbook-style writing gives you the freedom to choose the writing format you need to tell your stories. You'll soon become comfortable with these formats and will be able to quickly create dynamic, storytelling pages.

Bet You CAN and DO Write

As you read on you'll notice I've listed more than 20 formats for your journaling. Often I hear people say, "I can't write," but the truth is they do a lot of writing. They can't see themselves tackling a novel, that's all. But they'll write notes for the babysitter, lengthy letters inside Christmas cards and notes to the teacher. By helping you see all the ways you can write, I will prove that you CAN and DO write all the time.

By the way, don't get hung up on the names I've given formats. Instead, notice how many different ways exist to approach journaling in your scrapbook. One format might feature journaling written from the viewpoint of the scrapbooker. Another might be read as though the words come from the people in the pictures. Formats might be lengthy or sequential. Others might be short and skip around. Ideally, the finished writing will vary from page to page to support the stories you are trying to tell.

Any of the following formats or a combination of formats could work on any scrapbook page. You'll see examples of these formats throughout this book.

✔ **Bullet points**—short blurbs of information about the layout. These may or may not be full sentences. If the bullet forms a complete thought or sentence, punctuate the end. The "bullet" itself may be a reoccurring icon such as a heart, a star or an asterisk—or you may wish to use a small embellishment such as stickers or stamps.

Bullets work best for disconnected copy. Bulleted information that supports one theme might better be described as a list.

✔ **Lists**—informational copy pieces that are connected or related to each other, so that one central theme is supported. Again, these may or may not be full sentences. If they are, add punctuation.

Numbering listed items stresses the way each piece builds on the next. Furthermore, numbering can give you headline ideas such as "Six Ways to Tie My Shoes" or "My Child's 14 Favorite Snacks." Typically when a number is used at the beginning of a sentence,

Figure 8-1—**Herb Garden**. The kicker tells the story of how each move we've made has forced me to leave behind my herb garden. The words "herb garden" are both headline and the point of the extremely short story. Kickers add information and punch while letting the headline carry visual weight.

the number is written out in words. When a number is used within copy, numbers under 10 are written out (one, two, three, etc.) and numbers 10 and above are given as numerals (10, 11, 20, 150). However, these are journalistic style decisions and, as a scrapbooker, you decide what looks good to you.

As examples of lists you probably haven't considered scrapbooking, how about your grocery list? A packing list for a trip? Your daily to-do list? As your life changes, so do these lists.

✔ **Headlines**—the words used to announce or preview the information that appears on a page or pages. Periods are rarely used at the end of a headline. However, if the punctuation would be a question mark or an exclamation mark, include it as a way of letting your reader know the emotional context of your remarks.

Headline writers who work for print publication use present tense verbs in headlines. Journalism school teachers stress that a headline without a verb is really a caption in disguise. You don't need to worry about this distinction, but you may wish to play with using present tense verbs to see if this works for you.

Present tense verbs add action to your words. The more vivid the action verb, the more alive your writing.

✔ **Kickers**—small headlines that appear above the actual headline. Kickers bring a sense of fun or drama to a headline while supplying a dollop more of information. You could journal the kicker in a different font (type design) than your headline or even a different color. Always keep the point size (height of the letters) of a kicker smaller than the point size of your headline. Kickers line up with the left margin or appear centered over the headline.

✔ **Cutlines**—information (usually placed directly below or to the side of a photo) that explains what is happening and who is in the photo. Cutlines enjoy high readership. If you don't like writing, or if you are having a difficult time finding the room for a block of copy, a cutline may be all your page needs.

I like to group cutlines together, using abbreviations to explain which photo goes with which cutline. Denote "upper left" with UL, "lower left"

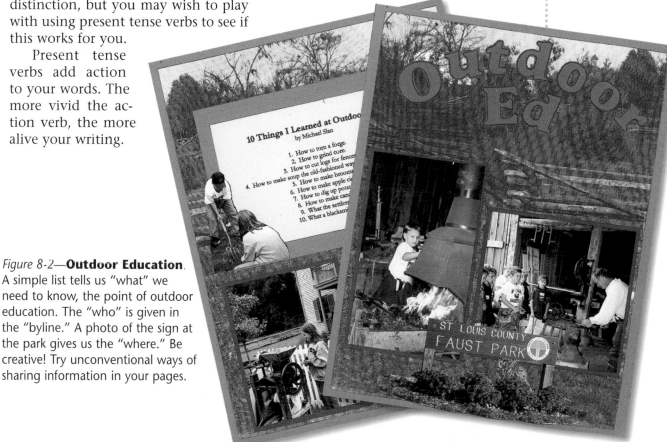

Figure 8-2—**Outdoor Education**. A simple list tells us "what" we need to know, the point of outdoor education. The "who" is given in the "byline." A photo of the sign at the park gives us the "where." Be creative! Try unconventional ways of sharing information in your pages.

with LL, "upper right" with UR and "lower right" with UL. These abbreviations can also be used to explain who's who within a photo. By grouping cutlines, the page design looks cleaner.

✔ **Captions**—comments made by the people or animals in the photos. Captions share captured smidgens of dialogue. By preserving exactly what people say, we give the reader the chance to experience the situation as we did. We also preserve a sense of the character who is speaking.

You may wish to put your captions in quotation marks to identify them as actual comments. While professional journalists only use one quotation mark ' ' to surround a caption in a headline, for scrapbooking this looks weird so I would probably use the standard double quotation mark " ", unless it takes up too much room.

If you write captions inside a quip balloon (the little white clouds cartoonists use to show that a character is talking), you don't need to use quotation marks unless the person talking is quoting another source. You can also indicate who spoke by simply putting a person's name at the end of the copy you have quoted. When you do that, changing the type style to bold or italic for the name only makes a nice visual statement.

✔ **Comment**—words you supply to remark about the pictured situation. Whereas a caption reflects the words of the person illustrated, comments reflect your thoughts or statements. For example, a page with a toddler might say, "Love this pacifier," using quotation marks to show these are the toddler's words. But, if you leave out the quotation marks, your page might say: Jason loves his pacifier.

The difference? A subtle shift of viewpoint. The ability to shift viewpoints gives you a chance to add variety, indicate personality and report with more accuracy who said what.

Figure 8-3—**Jungle Mike**. Captions, the remarks made by my son and the parrot, are in quotation marks. Comments, my remarks about the situation, stand alone. A ribbon of bright pink paper leads the eye through the spread. Crossbars of the green jungle print were used to tone down the brightness of the pink.

✔ **Dialogue**—information gleaned by recording the remarks of two or more people. Set apart the two speakers by using quip balloons, coloring the type differently, alternating type styles, alternating the colors behind the words, using quotation marks or separating the comments on the page.

Dialogue pages offer scrapbookers a way to give more than one person's viewpoint. Because scrapbookers work to save our whole family's memories, not just our own memories, dialogue pages add a lovely dimension to your scrapbook. When you view a dialogue page, you sense how families operate with a shared—but always personal—reality. (See Figure 5-8, page 61.)

✔ **Correspondence**—written communications. A handwritten note tells us so much about the writer! We note their stationery, handwriting style, choice of writing instruments, neatness, attention to detail and perhaps how their handwriting changed over time. Whenever possible, pair correspondence with a photo of the writer.

When I look over our family correspondence, I am fascinated by how one member never includes subjects in his sentences, preferring truncated phrases that look like this: "Haven't heard about your grades. Waiting for a response from your aunt. Need to talk to you about the holidays." Another always includes the latest updates on the natural world: "We had two little blue jays start coming to our bird feeder last week. They are so noisy! They chase off all the other birds with their nasty ways." Surely, there exists a way to analyze character from the shaping of our subject matter just as people analyze character from the shaping of our letters. (See Figure 3-7, page 36.)

✔ **Vital Statistics**—the bare necessities about the situation pictured. Typically, a date and a location appear, because the scrapbooker assumes the person in the photo is immediately recognizable. That last assumption may come back to haunt us.

For the sake of page design, vital statistics can be quietly tucked into a corner, or around a mat, under a picture, or across the bottom of a page. This nitty-gritty stuff does not need to

You may need to include in your journaling who the writer of the correspondence was by name or relationship.

*Figure 8-4—***Easter Bunny**. Inside the Easter basket is a short piece explaining that the Easter bunny had lots of places to hide eggs because we had just moved into our new house. Whenever possible try to go further than just commenting on the obvious.

announce its presence loudly on your page, but it does need to be there.

✔ **Lead**—an opening, descriptive sentence which usually relates the who, what, when, where and why. Typically the "lead" (pronounced "leed") would begin an article so that the reader quickly understood what she was reading about. If you only have space for two sentences, you might want to put the "when and where" and possibly the "why" somewhere on the page apart from the journaling.

You might use your journaling space to say: "Lizzie loved playing with the pine cones and the acorns. She pretended they were building blocks and made fairy furniture." Then, write the date and the place in a corner of the page. That might read: "Red Hills State Park, Indiana, October 20, 1999." If the story needs more detail, you may add another line under the date and place: "Rest stop on our way to Grandma Marie's house."

This "locator" information whispers the pertinent particulars without becoming the main focus of the page. Always ask yourself: "Who, what, when, where and why?" But remember which

portion of the answer you wish to emphasize.

If you are really pressed for space, or if the photos are self-explanatory, ask yourself: "Who, what, when, where and why?" and answer with as few words as possible. Put these words in a corner, journal them on a mat or journal them across the bottom of your page. Remember, they simply need to appear, but they don't need to demand attention.

✔ **Graph**—in journalese, this means a paragraph. If your subject warrants more detail, you can write several paragraphs, each two or more sentences long, to describe the action on the page. Once again, if you wish, you can split off the "when and where" if necessary to give yourself more room to write description. You can also split the graphs up, so that you have two areas of journaling. Depending on your layout, two journaled areas might be more pleasing to the eye than one.

✔ **Anecdote**—a very short story. Anecdotes usually have a beginning, a middle and an end, but these sections tend to be very, very brief. Typically anecdotes are amusing or interesting. If you write an anecdote of several paragraphs and decide to split the paragraphs up, make

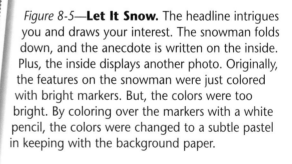

*Figure 8-5—***Let It Snow.** The headline intrigues you and draws your interest. The snowman folds down, and the anecdote is written on the inside. Plus, the inside displays another photo. Originally, the features on the snowman were just colored with bright markers. But, the colors were too bright. By coloring over the markers with a white pencil, the colors were changed to a subtle pastel in keeping with the background paper.

sure they are positioned in a logical manner so that the reader isn't confused.

✔ **Short Story**—a longer tale than an anecdote, and one that usually has several characters. Like an anecdote, short stories have beginnings, middles and ends. But, in a short story these sections are fleshed out. Furthermore, the middle of the story builds into a climax while the end resolves the crisis situation.

✔ **Family Story**—a story passed on which has been in the family for many generations—or that you wish to preserve for many generations. Listen for these when your family gathers for holidays or when your spouse puts a child to bed. Good family stories have a "tell-it-again" flavor to them. Children especially love family stories about their parents' youth. When you include a family story, the layout should include as many photos of the key character or items in the story as possible.

✔ **Journal**—a daily record of events. Information from a journal could be directly copied or edited for use on a scrapbook page. A journal differs from a diary because the journal tends to record events in the outer world, while a diary records our inner world. You may wish to supplement your journal with newspaper or magazine clippings about momentous events. When you transfer your journal writing to your scrapbook, you'll add photos and embellishments to make the page tell a story.

✔ **Diary**—a daily record of personal insights. Information from a diary should be used judiciously because most diary keepers do not intend their work to be published. However, your diary should yield plenty of raw material that can be edited for your scrapbook. You could also create a page styled after a diary page by headlining it "Dear Diary." Handwrite the copy and include the date. Tell the story as

> "I used to think that writing about myself in a journal was so vain. But over the years I have found that getting my thoughts on paper is rewarding in many ways. You're expressing what's inside of you, freely. Only then can you express yourself effectively to others."
>
> —**Helen Gurley Brown**

*Figure 8-6—***Janie's Big Fish**. The photo to accompany this family story was a tiny black and white from a Brownie camera. By enlarging the original photo, I was able to show much more detail and create a focal point for the layout. Although the headline gives the basics of the story, the left-hand page fills the reader on the funny little details.

Janie Caught a Big Fish—ME!

Grandpa Lindell took Janie and me fishing at a gravel pit somewhere in southern Indiana. He gave each of us a bamboo fishing pool, baited our hooks with worms, and went to talk with other fishermen nearby.

Now, the best part of a bamboo pole is how you can whip it back and forth in the air and make a swishing sound. So Janie and I stood on the bank whipping our poles around like Zorro.

All of a sudden, I felt a tension in my mouth. Then I felt a squirm. Janie's hook had caught me in the mouth and lodged inside my cheek. I tried to call out to her, but she was busy tugging on her pole—pulling me closer to h and digging the hook in deeper.

Finally, Grandpa noticed what was happening and unhooked me.

Janie caught a big fish—

ME!

Tip!

Put your name on the front or back of each page and the date it was completed. This may become significant information.

For example, all the women in my family scrapbook. I'd like to see us exchange our pages about Joshua, my nephew who died when he was four. If we added our names and dates, that would help us and our descendants discern our differing relationships with Josh.

though you were writing in your diary, but remember to edit your work since others will be reading your page.

✔ **Poem**—information set to rhyme or rhythm. The scrapbooker may rewrite familiar poems to be family specific or the scrapbooker might wish to compose original poetry. Others find poems which perfectly echo their sentiments and use them as part of a page. If you are fortunate enough to have a poem written by a family member, by all means use it! An old published poem written by my great-uncle forms the basis for a couple of wonderful heritage pages in my scrapbook. (See Figure 3-4, page 33.)

✔ **Quotation**—a quoted remark that has special meaning. You may wish to share the words of someone famous or the words a family member is famous for. In our family, we call a terrific parking place, "executive sparking." Silly, I know, but illustrative since the joke began when my husband circled a

mall parking lot for 20 minutes until the perfect space opened up. Now when a coveted place appears, we all chime out "executive sparking!" Simple rituals, special terms and inside jokes remind us we share our lives.

✔ **Reminiscence**—retelling a memorable instance from the past. Interview family members or write down what you recall about them. Then, if the piece is too long, edit it for inclusion in your scrapbook. When I edit a reminiscence, I like to keep the original with the edited version. Since plastic sheet protectors enclose my pages, the original can easily be slipped between two scrapbook pages. Building a pocket page offers another way to keep original with the edited version.

By the way, don't feel badly about editing a reminiscence. When Anne Frank's diaries first appeared, her father Otto Frank withheld several pages where Anne made observations about her mother and her parents' marriage. He did not, however, destroy those pages, and recently the diary has been re-released including them. All things have their time.

Don't forget to include your own reminiscences. Often scrapbook pages note the lives, thoughts and images of everyone in the family but the faithful scrapbooker. Occasionally, hand your camera to another person. Write down

Figure 8-7—**Princess Green Beans**. Putting away groceries sparked this memory of my little sister. Despite the amazed stares of the other people, I stood in Kinko's copying one green bean label after another. My son enjoyed hearing this story, and I was surprised to realize I'd never shared it with him. He was so tickled! Now I can be sure that this story will get passed on to the next generation.

your most memorable moments. Unfortunately, if we are too attentive to everyone else, they forget we had a life before they came on the scene.

✔ **Description**—a word picture of a situation or object. On occasion, you merely wish to explain what the viewer is seeing. Or, you may wish to add detail which can't be discerned from a photo or memorabilia. Descriptive passages can be short or long, depending on the amount of information you wish to convey.

✔ **Documentation**—a document that accompanied an object, situation or person. For example, you might wish to include a birth announcement on a page with a photo of your child. That would be documentation that you wrote or provided the information for. Other documents might include registration for a camp, change of address forms or a contract you signed. (See Figure 1-2, page 8.)

✔ **Recipe**—the instructions and ingredients for preparing food. What do you make that is your family's favorite? Is the recipe so simple that you could write it down off the top of your head? Devote a page to the recipe itself and photos of your family enjoying the finished product.

✔ **Portrait**—a short word picture that captures a person's personality. Added to a photo, this produces a well-rounded image. Include any habits, favorite sayings or unique traits of this person, because they may have more importance than you realize.

After his child was diagnosed with Tourette's Syndrome, one father realized that several members of his family had exhibited signs of same malady. "Now I have more compassion for these family members. I realize that they had the same challenges as my son—without the benefit of a medical diagnosis. I'm glad, though, that I remember them well enough to be able to assure my child that this does run in the family, and he will live a full life despite his problem."

Be sure to explain your relationship to the subject of your portrait. Otherwise, people who look at the page later, won't be able to distinguish family from non-family. Whenever

Remember to clear up information that may confuse those who come after you. For example, nicknames often mislead readers.

Michael and Madison Scott

My friend Michael Scott and his father made it a point to take at least one trip together each year. This photo was taken at The Lodge at Pebble Beach, California. You can see how proud Madison is of his son, and you also get a sense of Michael's energy and passion for life.

Figure 8-8—**Michael Scott**. On occasion, one photo does say volumes. This picture of my good friend, Michael Scott, with his father tells you so much about their relationship that all I needed to add was the details. Notice how the layout and colors support the sense of closeness and spirit in a masculine way.

With adopted children, foster children, step-children and other arrangements complicating the family line, why be restricted by traditional family trees? Instead, Joyce Maguire Pavao of the Center for Family Connections offers this alternative: family orchards. Along with the family tree, include those people connected to your family by love. Perhaps you could use different colored tree leaves to show blood versus affection connections.

possible, a sample of handwriting of the person you're writing about adds a nice extra dimension.

✔ **Memoir**—an account of someone or some happening that was notable. This would be longer than a reminiscence, which typically would cover one event. Think of those family members who have passed on. Write a brief memoir of each of them and send it to other family members asking for their additions or corrections.

✔ **A Family Tree**—Some novels begin with a page explaining who is related to whom and giving any nicknames that might be used. When your scrapbook is finished, why not go back through your pages and write down who is pictured, their relationship to you, their age at the time of the photo and any other pertinent information?

If you are one of the dear few friends who knew me before I turned 25, you have permission to call me "Jonie." If you are one of my father's friends or family, I'll even accept "Joni" as the spelling. If you are one of my friends from Decatur, Illinois, I'll answer to "Jo." Can you imagine how confusing this could be in a scrapbook? Let me add another dimension of intrigue: I am one of a long line of Joannas in my family, including my mother and my great-aunt. As you can see, a who's who would help future generations better identify exactly which Joanna is featured on the page.

In the same vein, be cautious when referring to "the war." As my mother wrote her memoirs, my sister keep stopping to ask, "Which war?" Reading your material out loud to your audience will help you spot these problematic areas.

*Figure 8-9—***Friendship with Shirley**. I borrowed my mother's memoirs to create these pages about her friendship with Shirley Helmly, my godmother. The closeness and ease these women feel comes across loud and clear in the photos. The "50 Years" emblem is repeated on each page as a reminder of how truly remarkable their friendship is. The pages close with an assortment of thoughts on friendship which echo the bond these two have created.

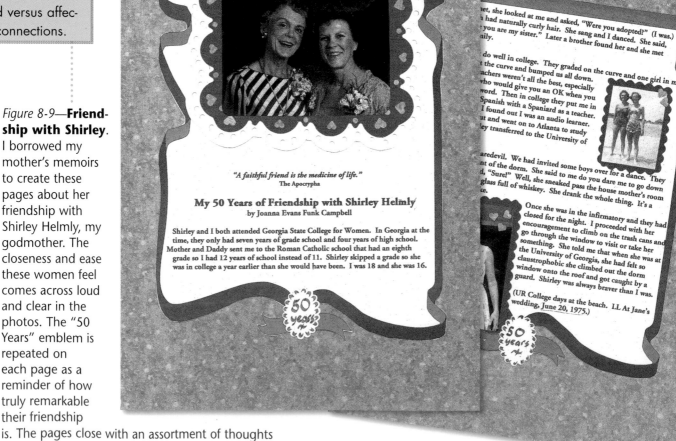

"A faithful friend is the medicine of life."
The Apocrypha

My 50 Years of Friendship with Shirley Helmly
by Joanna Evans Funk Campbell

Shirley and I both attended Georgia State College for Women. In Georgia at the time, they only had seven years of grade school and four years of high school. Mother and Daddy sent me to the Roman Catholic school that had an eighth grade so I had 12 years of school instead of 11. Shirley skipped a grade so she was in college a year earlier than she would have been. I was 18 and she was 16.

SAGE PAGE

The Handwriting is on the Wall, ...er, On the Page

Certainly you want to keep a sample of your loved ones' handwriting. However, there are advantages to rewriting handwritten memorabilia:

❑ **Editing**. You can edit the copy and make the information more clear and readable.

❑ **Ease**. You make the message more accessible if the rewriting is more legible.

❑ **Design**. You can reproduce the message in colored ink or a lettering style that better matches your page design.

❑ **Size**. You can make the message fit the space you've allotted for it.

Rewriting the materials does not mean destroying the originals. Here are a few ideas:

❑ **Pockets**. Store the memorabilia in a pocket on the page.

❑ **Crops**. Copy the memorabilia and crop the copy so that only a limited portion is exhibited on the page.

❑ **Slips**. Slip the memorabilia behind your page. This works well if you use plastic page protectors.

If you are concerned about the acid content of the memorabilia, copy or scan it onto archival quality paper. I tested my local color copier and found that the ink was acid-free.

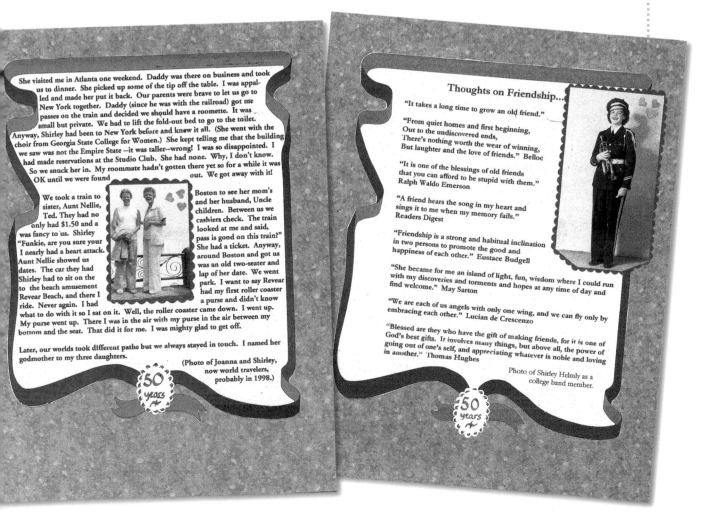

She visited me in Atlanta one weekend. Daddy was there on business and took us to dinner. She picked up some of the tip off the table. I was appalled and made her put it back. Our parents were brave to let us go to New York together. Daddy (since he was with the railroad) got me passes on the train and decided we should have a roomette. It was small but private. We had to lift the fold-out bed to go to the toilet. Anyway, Shirley had been to New York before and knew it all. (She went with the choir from Georgia State College for Women.) She kept telling me that the building we saw was not the Empire State –it was taller--wrong! I was so disappointed. I had made reservations at the Studio Club. She had none. Why, I don't know. So we snuck her in. My roommate hadn't gotten there yet so for a while it was OK until we were found out. We got away with it!

We took a train to Boston to see her mom's sister, Aunt Nellie, and her husband, Uncle Ted. They had no children. Between us we only had $1.50 and a cashiers check. The train was fancy to us. Shirley looked at me and said, "Funkie, are you sure your pass is good on this train?" I nearly had a heart attack. She had a ticket. Anyway, Aunt Nellie showed us around Boston and got us dates. The car they had was an old two-seater and Shirley had to sit on the lap of her date. We went to the beach amusement park. I want to say Revear Beach, and there I had my first roller coaster ride. Never again. I had a purse and didn't know what to do with it so I sat on it. Well, the roller coaster came down. I went up. My purse went up. There I was in the air with my purse in the air between my bottom and the seat. That did it for me. I was mighty glad to get off.

Later, our worlds took different paths but we always stayed in touch. I named her godmother to my three daughters.

(Photo of Joanna and Shirley, now world travelers, probably in 1998.)

50 years

Thoughts on Friendship...

"It takes a long time to grow an old friend."

"From quiet homes and first beginning, Out to the undiscovered ends, There's nothing worth the wear of winning, But laughter and the love of friends." Belloc

"It is one of the blessings of old friends that you can afford to be stupid with them." Ralph Waldo Emerson

"A friend hears the song in my heart and sings it to me when my memory fails." Readers Digest

"Friendship is a strong and habitual inclination in two persons to promote the good and happiness of each other." Eustace Budgell

"She became for me an island of light, fun, wisdom where I could run with my discoveries and torments and hopes at any time of day and find welcome." May Sarton

"We are each of us angels with only one wing, and we can fly only by embracing each other." Lucian de Crescenzo

"Blessed are they who have the gift of making friends, for it is one of God's best gifts. It involves many things, but above all, the power of going out of one's self, and appreciating whatever is noble and loving in another." Thomas Hughes

Photo of Shirley Helmly as a college band member.

50 years

Gibb's Hill Lighthouse

9 Polishing Your Stories

Unless you write regularly and frequently, you may never have experienced the clarity and insight that comes with writing. Until you've gone through several drafts of an article, you haven't known the pleasure of turning mush into substance. So, let me break it to you gently: all that is lovely and of value in writing begins as a jumbled mess of words.

When considering how to approach *Writing to Learn*, William Zinsser said, "I thought of how often as a writer I had made clear to myself some subject I had previously known nothing about by just putting one sentence after another—by reasoning my way in sequential steps to its meaning. I thought of how often the act of writing even the simplest document—a letter, for instance—had clarified my half-formed ideas."

In contrast to Zinsser, you'll usually know quite a bit about your subject. Yet, when you look back over your writing, you may feel a sense of disappointment. That's normal. But until you have that amorphous lump, until you have something to work with, you can't polish and perfect your writing. So, viva la lump!

The goal of this chapter is to help you turn that gooey stuff into prose. Consider this a crash course in editing. Please note, editing your own work presents more challenges than editing the work of others. Be patient with yourself.

The more you read the better you will write. Busy people can carve out additional time to read by listening to books on tape.

I love to listen and scrapbook because it's like having someone read to you while you work. You can borrow tapes from the library or grocery store, pop them in while you cut and paste, and enjoy the magic of mind theater. Reading—even being read to—introduces your brain to new words, phrasing, pacing and plotting. As a bonus, your kids will enjoy the tapes right along with you.

First Edit: Scan and Ask, "Does My Writing Work?"

After you have created your first draft, put the piece aside. Then, read what you have written again, asking yourself, "Does it work? What have I written here?" In other words, does the piece make sense and does it accomplish what you were hoping?

Run through these questions to help you decide if your first draft makes the grade:

✔ **Capture**: Did you get down the essentials of what happened?

If you are having trouble with capture, maybe you need to make more notes for raw material. Remember to journal or jot snippets down in a notebook. These are raw pieces of material which you will later use to create more extensive memories. Be sure to capture significant words or data so you won't have to rely on memory.

✔ **Collection**: Have you organized your thoughts? Does the written material make sense? Is there a central and strong focus? When horseback riding, you collect the horse before approaching a jump. Collection signifies an organized, directed effort.

✔ **Commentary**: Did you share what you feel about the situation? Did you give the reader a sense of why this was important to you? You can express emotions with punctuation, word choice or by simple description.

✔ **Condensation**: Have you culled out the unnecessary or repetitive? Make every word count by going through your work and cutting extraneous words. Remember, your photos will add the details to the scene.

> "...Everybody who is human cannot say a sentence without revealing something—something mild or violent or waggish in their souls—or without having something fine in it."
>
> —**Brenda Ueland**
> *If You Want to Write*

*Figure 9-1—***Sisters***. An example of condensation and capture at their essence. The photos tell what we were doing, the journaling tells who, when, where and why. Dark paper has a particularly dramatic appeal, spotlighting my bridal apparel and our faces. The silk flowers add texture, color, dimension and eye flow. Notice the overlapping which pulls all the elements together.

✔ **Composition**: How does the piece read? Read it out loud and notice any awkward points or stumbling blocks. If you have trouble reading what you wrote, rewrite it as if you were talking to a friend. The journaling should sound like you, on paper. If the words you write are not words you would speak, revisit your efforts.

Second Edit: Tricks of the Trade

As with all skills, as you progress in your writing you internalize certain "tricks of the trade" which immediately improve your work. These writing tips accelerate your growth as a wordsmith. Try incorporating these new skills in one of two ways:

❑ Read through the tips, focus on one at a time and master that before moving on.

❑ Write a first draft of your information in the format you think best. Do a quick scan as explained above. Review the writing as you go over the tricks of the trade listed as following. Make changes as desired with a goal of improving your skill level.

Now for the tricks:

✔ **Write to add value**. Ask the big, "So what?" Don't write what is obvious to the person looking at the page. Train yourself to add value by thinking "capture" instead of "write." Visualize details slipping away, and ask yourself what you need to stop from fleeing.

✔ **Show don't tell**. Use words to paint pictures. Allow people to experience what you did. My friend Lou Heckler explains this as "being the bank robber not the camera."

For example, I could tell you the weather scared me. Or, I could tell you the wind was blowing so hard the trees bent in half, the rain pelted the roof like golf balls and the temperature dropped 30 degrees in five minutes. Which made you more concerned about the weather?

When we tell people, we automatically awaken the tiny voice in all of us who says, "Oh, yeah? Prove it to me." When we show people, we invite them to experience a situation with us.

Tip!

Read your work out loud. Share this technique with your children, too, and watch their composition skills soar. After the oral sharing, ask yourself or them, "Would I actually say this in real life?" Notice that most punctuation follows normal pauses in speech. If you pause, check to see if you've included adequate punctuation at the same spot.

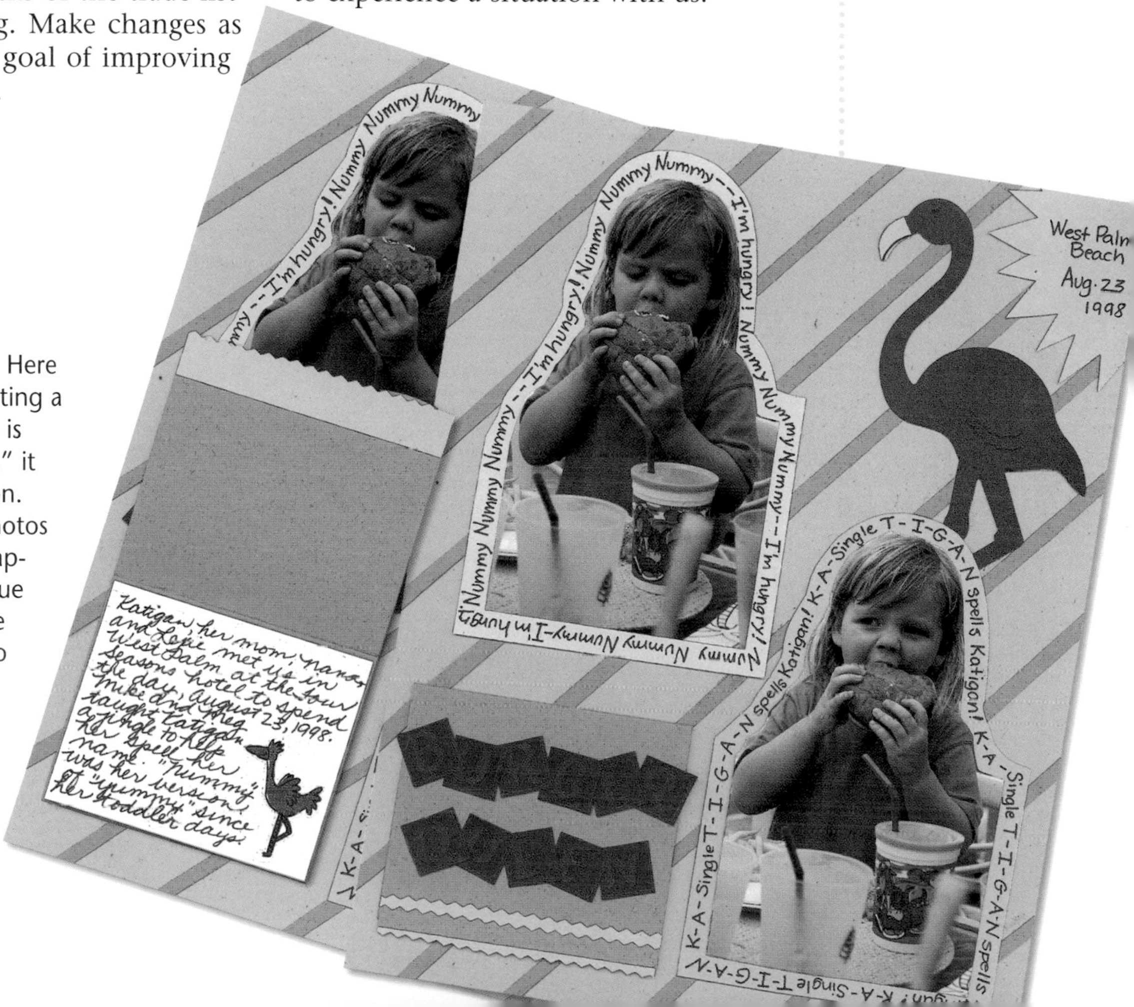

*Figure 9-2—**Burger Queen**. Here you see my niece Katigan eating a hamburger. If I wrote, "Here is Katigan eating a hamburger," it wouldn't add any information. Instead, I used these cute photos as a chance to record and capture information that is unique to Katigan. I wrote down the song her parents made up to help her learn to spell her name. Then, I wrote down the phrase "Nummy, nummy, nummy" which is her version of "Yummy, yummy, yummy." She's been saying that since she could talk.*

> "The writer has to devise a form for his inspiration which will at once please us as an artistic pattern and give us a convincing impression of disorderly reality. In addition to reconciling fact and imagination, he must reconcile fact and form. It is a hard task."
>
> **—Lord David Cecil**

✔ **Use transitional expressions**. Readers need to be led from one topic to another by the hand. Good connectors provide coherency to our words. Use transitions like:

then, when, if, because, but, however, conversely, on the other hand, in retrospect, fortunately, happily, sadly, to be honest, to say the least, perhaps, clearly, frequently, often, seldom, after, before, meanwhile, later, further, at this point, at the present time, as a result, for these reasons, also, again, too, likewise, furthermore, in addition, but, yet, during, concurrently, for example, in other words, similarly, simultaneously, at the same time, at another time, first, second, third, finally, last, eventually and instead.

These words establish relationships among ideas.

✔ **Bigger isn't better**. Often the perfect word exists somewhere out there. In your search for that word, don't fall prey to a word so uncommon and so pompous that your reader is stumped. If the right word eludes you, fill in the space with ******** and come back to the place later. Your subconscious mind continues to work on the blank while you move ahead.

✔ **Avoid adverbs**. Whenever possible, use strong verbs instead. These verbs tantalize the reader with their freshness and precision.

Weak—Joey would run quickly around the bases.
Strong—Joey would race around the bases.

Weak—Mary walked slowly across the parking lot.
Strong—Mary sauntered across the parking lot.

✔ **Use active construction**. Reword sentences reading "the this was done by the that." Instead, use the word after the "by" as the subject of your revised sentence.

Weak—The ball was hit by the pitcher.
Strong—The pitcher hit the ball.

Figure 9-3—**Ketchup Sandwich**. A funny story is captured on the "sandwich bread" inside the lunch bag. I also listed Michael's favorite foods on the "bread" since they seem to change so quickly. The drippy lettering on ketchup draws your eye and ignites your curiosity.

Weak—The project was recommended by the board.
Strong—The board recommended the project.

✔ **"To be or not to be" is to be shunned**. Avoid sentences with "It is..." or "There are..." construction. Choose specific action verbs or re-arrange the sentence.

Weak—There is a house sitting on top of the hill.
Strong—The house sits on top of the hill.

Weak—It is important to Joey that the team wins.
Strong—Winning is important to Joey.

✔ **Proper references required**. Pronouns refer to the closest noun in the preceding sentence. Check your sentences for clarity when using a pronoun or you will confuse your reader.

Weak—The dog and Dana both ran after the ball. Then she ran back with the dirty toy in her mouth.
Strong—Dana and the dog both ran after the ball. Then the dog ran back with the dirty toy in her mouth.

Weak—It has been reviewed by the committee, and it decided not to endorse the bill.

Strong—The committee reviewed the bill and decided not to endorse it.

✔ **Give specifics**. Particulars signal credibility to a reader. *USA Today* and *The Readers Digest* both pioneered articles thick with numbers, terminology and expert opinions.

Weak—A lot of people turned out to see the Pope in St. Louis.
Strong—One hundred and four thousand people attended mass with Pope John Paul II in the TWA Dome in St. Louis.

Weak—A blue bird flew from the tree to our feeder.
Strong—An indigo blue bunting flew from the maple tree to our feeder.

✔ **Quit using clichés**. The dictionary defines a cliché as a trite or overused phrase. In headlines, clichés can be entertaining. In copy, clichés offer space-filling emptiness. "A good time was had by all" lacks the infor-

> "I have made a great discovery. What I love belongs to me. Not the chairs and tables in my house, but the masterpieces of the world. It is only a question of loving them enough."
>
> **—Elizabeth Asquith Bibesco**

*Figure 9-4—***Indianapolis Dino**. A posed picture gives you great freedom to share a story or anecdote. In this case, the story was only a paragraph long, so I had room to add a memorabilia pocket to include the ticket into the museum. When you write your story, transitions help you move through time in a logical manner. This paragraph used "so, when, until, then" to organize the action.

mation you get from "we agree this was the best party we'd ever given."

✔ **Explore with the senses**. Sensory details invite the reader to share our experiences. As you write, think of linking your topic to your senses:

Smell—What did autumn smell like? Examples—burned leaves, soggy soil and apples.

Touch—What did the baby's head feel like? Examples—velvet, chick down, a powder puff.

Taste—What did the broken lip taste like? Examples—metal, salt, blood.

Sight—What did the sky look like? Examples—whipped cream, cotton balls, wisps of hair.

Sound—What did the hike sound like? Examples—breaking twigs, crunching leafs, sucking mud.

✔ **Be a trained noticer**. Humorist Jeanne Robertson uses the term "trained noticer" to describe a person who takes note of life's quirky details. When we share the fine points, we deftly change our readers' viewpoint from one-dimensional to multi-di-

mensional. Good fiction writers rely on details to develop characters.

For example, two crime authors, Sue Grafton and Janet Evanovich, both use food as a way to describe their sleuths. Grafton's character, Kinsey, is an orphan who gobbles down fast food in her car. Evanovich's character, Stephanie, is a striving-to-be-independent-single who regularly shows up at her parents' dinner table for homecooked meals, desserts and enough leftovers to last until the next visit.

Now, think of the members of your family. You've got your person who eats one food at a time, your person who uses ketchup as a universal cloaking agent, and your person who cuts everything on the plate into teensy pieces before eating. Not exactly enough information to develop an FBI profile, but nonetheless delightfully telling in a bizarre way.

✔ **Mark the trail**. Native Americans marked trails through the countryside for those who would come later by piling up rocks in certain formations. Successful writers mark trails for their readers to make the journey more pleasant. Using paragraphs as building blocks for your work:

> "To date, there have been at least nine small studies confirming that laughter boosts immunity and keeps it humming for a full day or more."
> —**Russell Wild**

Figure 9-5—**Over the Hill**. Let your reader's senses share your experiences. The sentence "cake shaped like a graveyard" gives a vivid visual impression while it implies a tasty treat. Note, too, that these photos are arranged sequentially from left to right. So, the story is told in words and in images. The red silk paper behind the three photos "collects" the story and guides our eyes.

❏ **Start with the overview**. Open with an umbrella statement giving the reader a general idea of what is to come, perhaps detailing the thoughts to be explored.

❏ **Develop a specific thought**. Take one thought and expand it.

❏ **Then develop another thought**. Expand it.

❏ **Finally, summarize**. The final sentence should tie up loose ends and offer a conclusion.

Here's an example:

Umbrella sentence—I had always wanted to go to England, and the opportunity presented itself when my friend Elaine was invited to London to make a presentation.

Development 1—When I jokingly mentioned my envy, she invited me to come along.

Development 2—A quick check of the calendar assured me the date was open.

Development 3—She checked to see if we could share accommodations.

Development 4—Finally, a talk with the airline confirmed I had enough frequent flier points to make the trip at no charge for airfare.

Summary—So, on March 26, 1999, my dream came true when Elaine and I boarded TWA flight 720 for London's Gatwick Airport.

✔ **Once upon a time, there was a beginning, a middle and an end**. Remember, you are a storyteller. If you think back, every classic fairy tale can be divided into those three discrete zones. The force of nature that decreed ants have six legs has also demanded that all stories have three parts. Deviating from the pattern will confuse your reader and weaken your tale.

Realizing the import of this story threesome, you can add tension by upping the ante during the middle of your saga. For example, you are writing about a disastrous happening on the way to church. You'll have my attention if you tell me this service was special because you were singing a solo in the choir. You'll have my sympathy if you tell me a run appeared in every

Check out James A. Michener's *Writer's Handbook*. The book explores how Michener rewrote his way to success. Michener shares nine short excerpts of editorial work detailing the eight times he rewrote his material. He says, "Taken together, they show how difficult it sometimes is to express an idea accurately, and how it has to be slaved over until it is expressed in acceptable language."

Figure 9-6—**Happy Birthday to Michael!** It's only two sentences long, but this story has a definite beginning (he woke up at 6:30 a.m.), middle (I've waited all year for this day) and end (most people don't eat snowcones for breakfast). Notice this paper is the same as the paper used in Figure 7-4, page 81. By emphasizing different colors within the paper, the page seems different.

pair of your hose. But you'll have me holding my breath if you tell me you ran a stop sign and looked up to see a policeman following you with his sirens blaring.

Notice how the drama heightened with each new problem. A good opening bodes well. A well-crafted middle with increasing tension glues the reader to the page. A great ending delivers the goods. By touching all three bases, you deliver a homerun.

✔ **Develop an ear for revealing dialogue**. The key word here is revealing. Blow-by-blow dialogue can be tedious. For example:

> "Let's have a picnic," said Molly.
> Sarah said, "What a good idea."
> Molly said, "I'll get the basket."
> "I'll make sandwiches," said Sarah.

None of this dialogue reveals information or insight about Molly and Sarah. They could be any two people at any age.

Instead, look for the small hidden jewels of normal. You can train yourself by reading articles and circling the direct quotations you find enlightening. Reading books of quotations will also heighten your sensitivity to revealing phrases.

When you hear a striking comment, scribble it down as fast as possible. Exact wording matters when trying to capture personality. Then, each word has impact. By including these delicious morsels, you'll better share the cast of today with the audience of tomorrow.

Weak (without dialogue)—Michael caught a toad on our late night walk and offered to let me keep it in my room.
Strong—Michael held the toad he caught on our late night walk and examined its bulging throat with awe. "Mom, this one sings so beautifully that I want to keep him in my room to sing me to sleep. And, if one night you are really lonely, I'll let you sleep with my toad in your room."

Notice how the rewritten passage tells you more about my son and his love of nature. Notice that in the rewritten version, the focus was on what actually was said rather than a description of Michael's offer.

Figure 9-7—**Love Song**. Here the paper and embellishments carry much of the visual telling of the story. The dialogue—which I jotted down immediately when we returned home—makes the tale "sing" with authenticity. Kids do say the darnedest things, as a page like this proves. Note that the photo wasn't even taken the same year as the story occurred. But, this page is more interesting than simply mounting the photo alone would have been.

Third Edit: Proofread Your Writing

✔ **Double-check your spelling**. Common words can fool us. You know those apples on a stick covered with a melted mixture of butter and sugar? Pronounce their name. Did you say, "Carmel apples?" Guess what? They are CARAMEL apples. Turn on your spell-checker or flip open your dictionary. A list of the most frequently misspelled words in English includes *accommodate, achievement, argument, believe, definitely, embarrass, exaggerate, February, necessary, occasion, occurrence, proceed, receive, remember, separate* and *tomorrow*.

Even the spell-checker won't save you from confusing *their*, *there* and *they're*. The solution? Keep a copy of the *Gregg Reference Manual* handy and refer to it often.

✔ **Usage can be tricky**. Be confident the word you choose correctly supplies the meaning you intended.

Wrong—She entered *forth* grade this year.
Right—She entered *fourth* grade this year.

Wrong—We were *anxious* to meet our new daughter-in-law.
Right—We were *eager* to meet our new daughter-in-law.

Wrong—Finally, we came to an agreement *between* the four of us.
Right—Finally, we came to an agreement *among* the four of us.

✔ **Play it again, Sam**. Rewriting perfects your drafts. Author Anne Lamott counsels us, "Almost all good writing begins with terrible first efforts." Put aside whatever mental image you have of a writer dashing off thoughts, ripping them out of the typewriter and handing them to a publisher. All writers write and rewrite.

While you won't be rewriting your journaling hundreds of times, I hope you'll experiment with rewriting your work at least once or twice. By doing so, you'll improve your skills, bring details into focus and craft meaningful family stories that will stand the test of time.

When proofreading, read your work from right to left. This oddball progression forces you to pay attention to each individual word. Otherwise, your brain glosses over irregularities, and you don't "see" your mistakes.

Figure 9-8—**Sweet William**. To make the Jewish Teaching fit in the small space on the page, I had to rewrite the sentence two or three times. The ability to rewrite copy easily is but one reason to do your initial journaling on computer, even if you later transcribe your composition in your album by hand. Other reasons to write on computer include availability of a spelling checker, readability, ability to change typefaces, ability to change print sizes and ability to print your words in color.

10 Assembling Your Pages

In past chapters we've looked at catching, preserving, illustrating, recovering, planning, formatting and polishing your family stories. In this chapter, you'll see how all these steps work together to create cherished family stories that will be as vivid two hundred years from now as they are today.

Before you get started, take a few moments to find a work location and collect the necessary materials.

Setting Up Your Work Space

To assemble your journaling, photos and embellishments, you need a clean and flat work space. If you use a kitchen table, like many of us do, be careful that no little spots of oil or food come in contact with your paper, or it will be ruined. Bright light will help you see what you are doing, and the best lighting will come from straight above you so there are no shadows. A nearby trash can will keep the area tidy, but a paper bag with the top rolled down and taped to your table will work, too.

I like to use a self-healing cutting mat under my work with a cardboard craft mat under that. The craft mat has a grid which helps me line up my elements. I covered the craft mat with clear plastic laminate to protect the surface from glue and to make the mat more durable.

Tip!

Don't toss those extra photos away. You can:

❑ Slip them inside your page protector behind the finished scrapbook page. They can stay there forever.

❑ Send them to other people who will enjoy them.

❑ Use them in another album, for instance, an album you make for your in-laws.

❑ Give them to your children so that they can scrapbook alongside you.

Pull Out Your Photos, Memorabilia and Mock Up

Even if you only drew a few squiggly lines, your sketches will guide your efforts. If you are copying a page from a book or magazine, get out the photo so you can look at it while you work. Or pull out your photos and memorabilia.

While I was working at a greenhouse in Muncie, Indiana, to put myself through college, Mr. Waldo taught me the fine art of culling. Go through your photos and select only the best ones. Organize your photos with the one you want to be dominant on top. Keep your protective photo sleeve nearby to slip your photos and memorabilia back inside if your work gets interrupted.

If the photos are too small or the memorabilia is too large, make color copies or scan the items and adjust the sizes. Making color copy enlargements turns a small photo into a stunning dominant image. When enlarging old

black and whites taken with Brownie cameras, you'll see a wealth of new detail previously hidden to the eye.

Selecting the Perfect Paper

Elements jell into a storytelling page when matted and backed with the right paper. Paper is the least expensive of all your scrapbook supplies, but the item that will add the most to your pages. Use only acid-free and lignin-free paper for your scrapbook.

Having sung paper's praises, let me issue a warning: Paper can mislead you. As you look at paper on racks or in books, realize that the paper that catches your eye may overwhelm your photos and overpower your journaling (see Figure 10-2, next page).

Don't allow the paper to dictate your page. Don't use that cute piece of Easter paper where the bunnies are bigger than your nephew. Push aside that stunning piece of wedding paper that makes the bride look pale instead of radiant. Instead of worrying about papers' themes, pay strict attention to papers' color, mood and pop.

❑ **Color**—Color never stands alone. When I wear gray, my eyes look gray. When I wear blue, my eyes look blue. When I wear green… you get the picture. Color responds to other colors. Your best results come from picking up

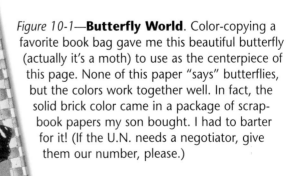

*Figure 10-1—***Butterfly World***. Color-copying a favorite book bag gave me this beautiful butterfly (actually it's a moth) to use as the centerpiece of this page. None of this paper "says" butterflies, but the colors work together well. In fact, the solid brick color came in a package of scrapbook papers my son bought. I had to barter for it! (If the U.N. needs a negotiator, give them our number, please.)*

colors that already occur in the photographs.

For guaranteed color success, remember the rule of *threes*. Limit yourself to no more than three colors and make sure each color appears three times. So, if your page is red, white and blue, the blue might appear on a mat, in the subject's clothes and in a sticker of the American flag. When you add an accent color that only appears once on the page, you have the beginnings of color confusion.

❏ **Mood**—Choose colors and prints that support your page's theme. Colors and prints speak subtly to our emotions. A busy toddler page calls for bold designs and primary colors. A snoozing child would look best surrounded in gentle images and pastels. A child playing in a swimming pool needs bright colors and striking shapes to emphasize the heat of summer. A little girl ready for her first Communion suggests somber colors and subtle designs to emphasize the event.

❏ **Pop**—Color and pattern work together to create backgrounds that enhance your photos or backgrounds that overwhelm your photos. When the background is right, the people in the pictures will visually "pop" off the page. If you've ever had your colors done, you understand the impact of color and design.

To see how "pop" works, try this experiment. Take a photo and hold it next to four or five different papers. As you move the photo from paper to paper, you'll see how one paper may truly emphasize your image and the others will do nothing for it.

If you have trouble finding the right paper for your page, take your photos into a scrapbooking supply store and hold the pictures next to different colors and prints. You'll be amazed at the difference your selections can make.

Working with Embellishments

Webster defines embellish as "to make beautiful with ornamentation." In scrapbooking, embellishments establish themes that tie together all the design elements of a page. They include stickers, die-cuts, punch art, borders, embossed designs, stamped art, templates, inked designs, coloring, ribbon, stenciling, tracings, textured elements, and rounded corners.

If you mat your photos, experiment with how the mat paper looks with the photo and the background paper. Sometimes you can use a background paper that doesn't pop by matting your photos and journaling generously with a paper that does pop.

Figure 10-2—**Little Britches**. Pop isn't just about color. It's about tones and shades and patterns, too. Originally, these photos were going to go on light blue paper. However, the wonderful warm tones of Michael's skin were chilled by the cool shades of blue. I tried several other combinations. The rich wood tones and the warm skin tones worked best with a warmer blue and a tan. You'll probably quickly see the other flaw in the page. I didn't leave myself room to journal.

This list will help you see the variety of themes possible using different scrapbooking tools:

Possible Themes

Stars, hearts, trees, cars, flowers, boats, airplanes, helicopters, eggs, rabbits, teddy bears, diaper pins, bottles, palm trees, pencils, military gear, circles, spirals, waves, sun, moon, flags, butterflies, school buses, ABCs, crayons, lighthouses, fish, paw prints, dogs, cats, birds, fish, footprints, handprints, bows, clock faces, splashes, rainbows, cowboy gear, horses, horseshoes, denim, gingham, sunflowers, children's silhouettes, storks, bees, postcards, postal stamps, umbrellas, buckets, shovels, plants, gloves, mittens, leaves, gingerbread people, paper dolls, maps, road signs, envelopes, diplomas, frogs, snakes, lizards, crocodiles, graduation caps and gowns, roses, flowers, crosses, X's and O's, church steeples, lip prints, lipstick, candy canes, candies, Hannukah, holly, wreaths, Christmas trees, Christmas tree lights, Christmas stockings, telephone, books, wild animals, scissors, cars, bicycles, circles, apples, dogs, rope, mountains, camping gear, fishing rods, Band-Aids, sea shells, insects, cartoon characters, earrings and pearls.

Embellishments to Illustrate Themes

- ❑ Templates
- ❑ Patterned papers used as mats
- ❑ Punch art
- ❑ Die-cuts
- ❑ Stickers
- ❑ Border stickers
- ❑ Border templates
- ❑ Border tape
- ❑ Stamped borders
- ❑ Rounded corners
- ❑ Art elements cut from acid-free paper (such as cutting out pictures from border paper)
- ❑ Photocopies
- ❑ Stencils
- ❑ Texture (such as crimping paper)
- ❑ Ribbons
- ❑ Dry embossing (using a tool to create a raised image)
- ❑ Wet embossing (adding embossing powder to an inked design)
- ❑ 3-D art objects (such as buttons)
- ❑ Dried flowers and leaves
- ❑ Punched out borders
- ❑ Spangles or sequins
- ❑ Feathers

Embellishments are to scrapbooks what accessories are to wardrobes. You wouldn't wear a pair of paper maché

> "In reality, we are obliged to improvise our happiness with such rough materials as fall to hand."
>
> —**Richard Schickel**

Figure 10-3—**Moods**. Papers and embellishments create moods that either support your theme and story or work against you. Here are four different moods: Romantic, featuring water-colors, pastels, flowers and lace; Fun, alive with bright colors, sharp images and simplicity; Country, showing soft colors, stencil-type patterns, quilting and a sense of the homemade; and Classic, displaying botanical correctness, naturally occurring patterns in granite, and handmade paper.

chili pepper earrings with an evening gown, would you? Why? Because you'd be mixing your moods.

Often, when we skip the page planning stage, we may be tempted to solve a design problem by slapping stickers all over the place.

If you're ever tempted to do this, ask yourself, "Is this a scrapbook or a sticker album?" If you can't tell, you've strayed from the path.

All embellishments create a mood, be it cartoonish or romantic. Mixing different styles of stickers or stamps confuses the mood.

On the other hand, using embellishments to establish a theme that supports your page's focus creates a strong undercurrent that strengthens your page's appeal.

It's Time for Tools

Every scrapbooker needs a see-through ruler, a pencil and eraser, good scissors, acid-free glue or photo splits, and an archival quality pen. A bottle of un-du™ or Goo Gone® Sticker Lifter™ will pay for itself quickly, so splurge!

With the un-du™ or Goo Gone® Sticker Lifter™ you can remove every element you adhere to the page without ripping your paper or photo. Squirt a small amount of this solvent onto the element you want to move,

use the supplied trowel-like tool to get under the element, peel off the element and let the solvent dry.

Buying new tools dramatically raises your scrapbooking investment. Before you make a purchase, attend a crop where you can borrow tools. You may discover you prefer an oval-cutter to a circle-cutter. Or that you can't line up the edges of specialty scissors to save your neck. Conversely, you might decide you can't live without a paper trimmer. At least when you make a purchase, you'll have experience to guide you.

Play with Your Elements

Once you've gathered all your photos, your journaling, your paper and your embellishments, try them in different arrangements on your page. Even if you've made a thumbnail, you have a chance to make alterations. Remember that one element must dominate the page. Plan for creating one page, two pages or more.

*Figure 10-4—**Daniéle Rose**. This page uses the theme of a rose, Daniéle's middle name. A purse takes center stage for focus because she loves purses, it underscores her "girly" nature and one of her habits is filling up old purses with stuff. (Habits like these are so easily forgotten.)

The rose supplies a theme to tie together all the elements of the page. Notice, too, that the color pink dominates the page. When planning the page, I had a photo of Daniéle that I liked but she was wearing clothes that clashed with pink. Just because you have a photo doesn't mean that you are duty bound to use it. Wait until you find its perfect place.

Tip!

To line up specialty scissors, make a template of the edging you want out of clear acetate. (I use transparencies for overhead projectors.) Use the template to trace the edge where you want the design to fall. Then line up the edge of the blade along your tracing marks and cut. Be sure not to cut to the end of the blade because the design usually doesn't extend all the way to the end.

To produce a pleasing page, you must control the eye movement of your viewer. Use one of five basic patterns to influence the way the eye travels.

1. **The vertical pattern** directs the eye up and down the page, using graphics, typography, lines and color. Your dominant element will be vertical. You might even run your headline up and down. (Don't forget you can crop a photo or arrange copy in a vertical pattern.)

2. **The horizontal pattern** directs the eye left to right across the page, using graphics, typography, lines and color. Your dominant element will be horizontal. Your photo, journaling or headline will go across the page.

3. **The diagonal pattern** takes the eye from one corner of the layout to the kitty corner. (How's that for a Southern Indiana word?) Your domi-nant element would have a photo, headline or journaling on an angle or a series of elements traveling from a lower corner across the page to the op-posite upper corner (see Figure 10-7, page 120). You often see diagonal pat-terns in scrapbooks when an 8 $\frac{1}{2}$" x 11" paper is tilted and pasted down on a 12" x 12" page (see Figure 7-7, page 84).

4. **The fractional pattern** divides the page into sections of differing val-ues. The dominant elements receive $\frac{2}{3}$ of the eye-dwell time. You can create a fractional pattern by putting a domi-nant element in the middle of the page, putting a dominant element on the left or right, or putting a dominant element on the top or bottom of the page. You can actually design a frac-tional page by dividing the working space you have in half, but using pat-tern or color to give one half of the page more intensity than the other.

Different patterns and textures have different optical weights. Let's think about how this works:

Light: Small patterns
Heavy: Larger patterns

Michael on a "dinosaur dig." Indianapolis Children's Museum

Figure 10-5—**Dino Mike**. This shows a horizontal layout that encourages the eyes to zigzag through the page. The dinosaur paper was so bold that it threatened to overwhelm the photos. So, I cut it into strips which lessened its optical weight by breaking it up. Note, too, that Michael always faces IN to the page, because your eyes follow his. The mats don't overwhelm the photos, but they do create a clear visual fence around the images. The photos were cropped to remove any further visual distractions.

Light: Subtle colors
Heavy: Bright colors

Light: High contrast (example black and white)
Heavy: Low contrast (gray tones)

Light: Small amount of lettering
Heavy: Dense lettering

Light: Open and airy type style
Heavy: Bold and/or condensed type style

Light: Broken up block of color
Heavy: Solid block of color

Light: Dots
Heavy: Stripes

Light: Repetitive design
Heavy: Bold design with few repeats

Once you understand how a fractional design works, you can see why pages patterned after quilting blocks work only part of the time. If the block features an equal number alternating shapes with the same optical density, the design has no eye flow. The resulting pattern will look neat and optically confusing at the same time.

A variation on the fractional design rule suggests we always use elements in odd number multiples. So, if you are putting stars on a page as an embellishment, use 3, 5, 7 or another odd number of them. The unevenness pleases the eye.

5. **The "bleed" design** focuses on a dominant graphic element that then bleeds off (extends off) the edge of the page. A common bleed design in scrapbooking occurs when a portrait photo is centered and surrounded with mats that extend to the edge of the page. Journaling is placed below or above the central graphic.

Within a page, you can direct eye flow with art elements. Stripes, diagonal lines within a photo, the direction of the eyes of the photo's subject, borders and shapes all contribute to eye movement.

Crop and Mat

Now you know what you want to go where, but how do you make it all fit?

Tip!

If you are having trouble coming up with a theme, close your eyes and visualize the person in the photo. What adjectives come to mind? For the page shown below, when I think of our friend Erin, the word "natural" comes to mind. Notice how the papers I used supported that theme. After I finished, I remembered that Erin is an Irish name and the color green figures predominantly on this page.

*Figure 10-6—**Prom**. Here is one version of a "bleed" design. By matting the photo on two realistic papers, the picture seems to bleed off the page by extending the visual image. Erin and her friend Jake demand our attention because people naturally gravitate to pictures of other people. To keep the headline and journaling in the same theme, I used watercolor pencils which picked up the colors of the plants and flowers. Then, I smeared the watercolor pencil with a damp cloth for a softly colored background.

Cropping cuts off unneeded or undesirable sections of a photo. Crop photos for these reasons:

❏ To make the photo fit the space.

❏ To cut off distracting backgrounds around the central figure.

❏ To emphasize part of the photo. This style of cropping is called "bumping." You might bump out a portion of a person to emphasize motion.

Don't be afraid to crop half an arm or a leg. The mind's eye fills in the rest of the figure. Remember that when you crop the background, the color of the photo may seem different. (Color never stands alone. A picture of a person wearing red in front of a green background will look different if you crop away the background and put the person on a blue mat.)

Don't crop precious photos, historic photos or Polaroid™ photos with the chemical packet at the bottom of the shot. Color-copy these photos so you can cut them without fear. If you don't want to crop a photo, but you do want to block out the background, put your mat over the top of the photo.

You can use a wide mat or a thin one, depending on the amount of room you have and how much emphasis you want to give to the mat.

A mat serves many purposes:

❏ A space on which to journal (see Figure 9-2, page 105).

❏ A visual "fence" between the photo or design element and the background paper (extremely important when you have a paper that might overwhelm your art element or photo).

❏ A color agent to tie the photo or design element to the rest of the page.

❏ A way to give an art element depth on the page—especially if you use a paper crimper (see Figure 8-8, page 99) or spacers to add height.

❏ A design technique to give elements more visual weight (see Figure 8-9, pages 100 and 101, note how a wide outside mat frames the narrow ribbon).

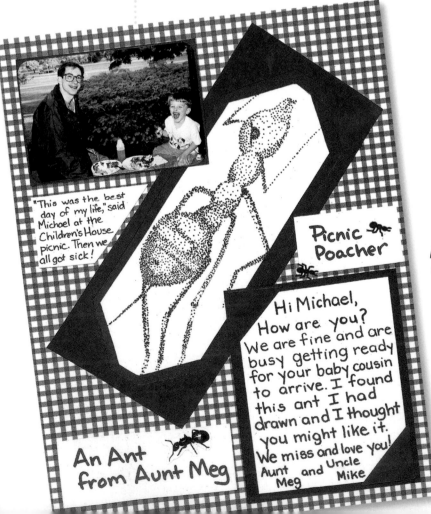

*Figure 10-7—***Picnic Poacher**. The ant forms a dramatic diagonal element on this page. Overlapping the photo and the journaling helps to pull the elements together. Notice that when journaling is given enough space, color and matting, it becomes a design element by virtue of its optical weight. Resist the urge to fill every space with stickers. As you can see, a little goes a long way. Too many small stickers clutter the page and confuse the eye.

Print Out Your Writing and Ink in Your Headline

You may need to adjust your journaling to make your page come together. (Actually, you can adjust the journaling first and do the cropping second, or vice versa. Each different page design may make one or the other a more obvious first choice.)

First, concentrate on the headline. Sketching the words on a sheet of tissue paper over the layout will help you see where the words should or could go. Is the size of the lettering workable? If not, you could trace the lettering and adjust the size on a copier. Does the style look good on the page? In general, the more complex the background is, the more simple your lettering style or font should be.

When creating a two-page spread, notice where the words will fall in relation to the gap between the pages. A huge gap breaks the visual impact of the words and looks weird. The best-looking headlines will divide themselves almost evenly on the two pages. For this reason, I like two- or four-word phrases where the words and spaces divide almost exactly in two.

Now, if you've done your journaling or writing on a computer, you can easily adjust the copy to fit the space you wish to fill. Printing your copy in colored ink that compliments your mats or background paper adds a nice touch.

If you wish to do your journaling by hand, first write your copy in pencil, then go over it with archival ink. Let the ink dry, then erase the pencil and use a cheap paint brush to brush away the eraser crumbs.

Other Places to Put Your Journaling

What if despite our best plans, you discover you have more writing than space? Besides putting your journaling in a copy block (a solid shape of text), you have many creative places to add your stories. Here are a few:

❑ On wide mats around the photos.

❑ Inside die-cuts.

❑ Around the outside page border.

❑ Beneath the photos.

❑ In caption balloons or bubbles.

> "Into my mind came words I had over-heard long before, when a young friend was being lectured by his father. 'Son,' the father said grandly, 'here's a lesson you might as well learn right now: Life is not just a chair of bowlies.'"
>
> **—Mary Engelbreit**

*Figure 10-8—***Chair of Bowlies**. Mats can go behind a photo or on top of the photo. In this case, since the photos were old, the mat rests on top to frame the pictures. (This mat was made by putting together strips of paper to form a frame.) Because dots are such a clean pattern, they don't fight with my small presence in the photos. The look is simple and clean even though this page actually uses six different papers, not counting the green plant accents.

- Inside a page pocket (see Figure 6-7 page 73).

- Inside a design element (see Figure 9-3, page 106).

- Behind a photo or as a design element (see Figure 9-6, page 109).

- Under a design element (see Figure 10-1, page 114).

- On a facing page (see Figure 3-11, page 40).

- Under a hinged element of the page (see Figure 3-7, page 36).

- On a pull-out element of the page (see Figure 10-9, below).

Once you decide that including your writing adds value to your scrapbook, you'll look for exciting ways to put storytelling words on your pages.

Tack It All Down

Your very last step is adhering all your design elements to the page. Before you begin any gluing or taping, place the elements on the page the way you want them. Please note, when I say "gluing, taping or pasting," I am referring to adhering design elements to each other or the page with archival quality adhesive.

Here are some names of common adhesives followed by their purposes.

Neutral pH Adhesive by Lineco—to bind together punch art pieces. (Use a toothpick or a small brush.)

Photo Stickers by Fiskars—commonly called photo splits, use these to mount photos or memorabilia.

2 Way Glue by Zig Memory System—to temporarily adhere pieces or for permanent attachment of medium-sized pieces.

Mono®Adhesive by American Tombow (permanent or temporary)—to mount large pieces or bind large pieces together. (This tends to get stringy like mozzarella cheese. If you get a piece gummed up on the outside of an element, use a dab of un-du™ or Goo Gone® Sticker Lifter™ on a rag to wipe the glue off.)

Figure 10-9—**Mia**. The image of my friend Kathy's daughter is so pure, that I didn't want my journaling to attract attention. I took great care to match the colors on this page. At first glance, you might think "pink," but the color of the roses is actually peach. A note to the baby tucks inside the pocket.

Acid-Free Photo and Document Mending Tape by 3M—to secure loose ends on the back of a page. Great for large areas. You can also repair torn photos or paper by adhering this to the back of the tear.

Start by gluing small pieces to larger pieces, because the larger the piece the easier it is to handle. (And, you're less likely to lose large pieces than to lose small pieces.)

Paste your page elements down working from the bottom to the top. If you make a mistake, use the un-du™ or Goo Gone® Sticker Lifter™ to remove the elements without ripping the paper.

Put It in a Page Protector

Cut a piece of waxed paper twice the size of your page. Wrap the wax paper around the page like a sleeve. Slip the bottom edges of waxed paper inside the open edge of the page protector. Slide the finished page into the page protector. Admire your work! Share it with your friends and family.

A Few Parting Thoughts...

While writing this book, I made many color copies of the scrapbook pages. Each time I went to Kinko's, one or two people would stop to look at my work. So often they would say, "I'd love to do that!" And I would encourage them. That's the purpose of this book: encouragement. What you have to say, the life you live, the values you hold are important, perhaps more so today than ever.

Maybe you, like me, live a simple life. My world revolves around my family, my friends and my faith. When I work on my scrapbook, I pay homage to all I care about. I am reminded of how blessed I am. I hope that you, too, feel that same sense of joy on your quest to preserve your family stories.

> "Whatever it is, there is a remarkable force called life that needs to be greeted with honor, decency and courage. And that no matter what field you're in, if that is how you choose to embrace life, you might find that you live life in the richest way you can possibly live it."
>
> **—Harry Belafonte**

*Figure 10-10—***Turtle Park***. Using a photo of a turtle for the pattern in the center, I created this puzzle page of Michael and his friend, Peter. Good thing I didn't glue anything down right away, because I must have made a zillion adjustments to get the area between the photos to come out.*

We chose to end the book with this page for many reasons. One is because this park is dedicated to children everywhere, and we'd like to dedicate this book to families everywhere. Another reason is that this park is just one of the many free attractions our great city, St. Louis, has to offer. And last, but not least, we hope that scrapbooking will bring out your sense of playfulness and creativity.

Now... go forth and scrap!

BONUS Figure—**Fortunate Family**. While cleaning up after Chinese take-out, I decided to create this interactive page. We had kept our fortunes, but you could easily create your own. During the Chinese New Year, folks exchange red envelopes with money inside for "good luck." Although I made the red envelope, you could easily use a red acid-free envelope.

Page Chart

How to use this chart: I have evaluated the difficulty of these pages by taking into account both the journaling and the scrapbook techniques required. An "Ease" level of "1" indicates the easiest to do, and a "3" is the most time-consuming.

All pages (except Figures 5-5 and 5-6 created by Michael Slan) were designed and created by Joanna Campbell Slan.

Figure I-3—**Great Big Brownie Smile**
Pg. 3   Ease: 1   Size: 8 ¹/₂" x 11"

Skill or Technique:
✔ minimal journaling, headline only
✔ hand-drawn brownie
✔ color copies of trefoil and badge sash
✔ heritage page
Supplies: Brown Plaid paper by Paper Pizazz; pencils by Berol; markers by Zig

Figure I-4—**Soccer It to Me**
Pg. 4   Ease: 3   Size: 8 ¹/₂" x 11"

Skill or Technique:
✔ extensive journaling and capturing dialogue
Supplies: Paper by Paper Patch

Figure 1-2—**Love at First Sight**
Pg. 8   Ease: 2   Size: 12" x 12"

Skill or Technique:
✔ intermediate journaling
✔ use of memorabilia
✔ traced art
✔ production assistance by Dr. Barry Slotky
Supplies: Paper by Hallmark; Watercolour pencils by Derwent

Figure 1-3—**Katigan**
Pg. 9   Ease: 1   Size: 8 ¹/₂" x 11"
Skill or Technique:
✔ minimal journaling
✔ using paper crimper
✔ sticker paper cut into diagonal strips
✔ punch art
Supplies: Sandy Lion Stickers

Figure 1-4—**Star-Struck (before)**
Pg. 10   Ease: 1   Size: 12" x 12"
Skill or Technique:
✔ minimal journaling, headline tiles
Supplies: Stickers by Frances Meyer, Inc.; Hallmark border stickers; Fontastic! type

Figure 1-4—**Star-Struck (after)**
Pg. 10   Ease: 2   Size: 12" x 12"

Skill or Technique:
✔ intermediate journaling
✔ heritage page
✔ use of memorabilia and die cuts
Supplies: Edge Accents™ scissors by Paper Adventures; markers by Zig

Figure I-5—**Busy as Beavers**
Pg. 11   Ease: 3   Size: 8 ¹/₂" x 11"

Skill or Technique:
✔ extensive journaling in newsletter style
✔ art from advertising in magazine
Supplies: Natural Pine paper by Provo Craft

Figure 1-6—**Michael's First Menorah**
Pg. 12   Ease: 2   Size: 8 ¹/₂" x 11"

Skill or Technique:
✔ intermediate journaling, capturing a frightening moment
✔ copying a fragile paper keepsake
Supplies: Paper by Paper Pizazz; scalloped scissors by Paper Adventures

Figure 1-7—**Tulips***Two Friends**
Pg. 13   Ease: 1   Size: 11" x 8 ¹/₂"

Skill or Technique:
✔ intermediate journaling
✔ using computer for scrapbooking
✔ using tulips to mat postcards
✔ tile lettering with tulip shapes
Supplies: Creative Photo Albums

Figure 2-1—**Snow Much Fun**
Pg. 16   Ease: 2   Size: 8 ¹/₂" x 11" spread

Skill or Technique:
✔ intermediate journaling
✔ stamping technique (embossing added to trunk; white opaque marker added to limbs for snow)

✔ color copying of photos at intervals increasing by 30 percent each time
Supplies: To Die For lettering from *LMNOP* by Lindsay Ostrom & Friends; stamp of tree by Stampa Rosa

Figure 2-2—**Angel Encounter**
Pg. 18   Ease: 1   Size: 8 ¹/₂" x 11"

Skill or Technique:
✔ editing, preserving a family memory
✔ light box tracing of letters in headline
✔ cutting and moving printed angel images
Supplies: Paper by The Paper Company; Clouds paper by Paper Pizazz; stickers by Mrs. Grossman's

Figure 2-3—**Goodbye, England's Rose**
Pg. 19   Ease: 2   Size: 8 ¹/₂" x11"

Skill or Technique:
✔ intermediate journaling of a "never forget" from history
✔ light box traced lettering
✔ double mat
✔ punch art rose and leaves
Supplies: Muted Roses and Peach Moire papers by Paper Pizazz

Figure 2-4—**Mark McGwire**
Pg. 21   Ease: 2   Size: 8 ¹/₂" x11" spread

Skill or Technique:
✔ intermediate journaling, capturing a child's viewpoint of history
✔ matted written copy
✔ pop-up ball made by crisscrossing two strips of paper to form "spring"
Supplies: Lettering Template by Frances Meyer, Inc.; photos of Busch Stadium and Mark McGwire by the *St. Louis Post-Dispatch*; Cover of *St. Louis Post-Dispatch*

Figure 2-5—**House in Champaign**
Pg. 22   Ease: 3   Size: 8 $\frac{1}{2}$" x11" spread

Skill or Technique:
✔ intermediate journaling plus quotation
✔ paper woven into lattice
✔ cut out embellishments from corresponding paper
Supplies: Paper by the Paper Patch

Figure 2-6—**Acorn Theory**
Pg. 23   Ease: 2   Size: 8 $\frac{1}{2}$" x11"

Skill or Technique:
✔ intermediate journaling and use of family correspondence
✔ heritage photo
✔ tree hand drawn, colored with pencils
Supplies: Paper by NRN Design; stickers by Hallmark; colored pencils by Berol

Figure 2-7—**Memories of Josh**
Pg. 24   Ease: 2   Size: 8 $\frac{1}{2}$" x11" spread

Skill or Technique:
✔ extensive journaling, capturing memories
✔ memorial page
✔ using stationery
✔ using a quotation
Supplies: Paper by Flavia Publishing (customized by author); markers by Zig

Figure 3-2—**Read to Me**
Pg. 31   Ease: 3   Size: 12" x 12"

Skill or Technique:
✔ extensive journaling, listing child's favorite books
✔ stationery color copied and enlarged for book's embellishment
✔ created fake book with gold lettering
✔ used hole punch to make insides of open letters
Supplies: Crow's Feet (Green) by Paperabilities III; Lettering Template by Frances Meyer, Inc.

Figure 3-3—**The Sixties**
Pg. 32   Ease: 3   Size: 12" x 12" spread

Skill or Technique:
✔ extensive journaling; use of references plus interview with Mary Ellen Burford
✔ Internet use of art and photos
✔ punch art
✔ stickers
✔ heritage page
✔ use of memorabilia
Supplies: Bluebird sticker by Frances Meyer, Inc.; markers by Marvy

Figure 3-4—**Edward Manigault**
Pg. 33   Ease: 3   Size: 8 $\frac{1}{2}$" x11" spread

Skill or Technique:
✔ extensive journaling and interviewing
✔ punch art
✔ photocopy of original poem and photo by F. Manigault
Supplies: Paper by Amscan; paper by Frances Meyer, Inc.; Leaf punch by Family Treasures

Figure 3-5—**Camera Shy**
Pg. 34   Ease: 1   Size: 8 $\frac{1}{2}$" x11"

Skill or Technique:
✔ minimal journaling
Supplies: Paper by Paper Patch; lettering template and stickers by Frances Meyer, Inc.

Figure 3-6—**Tony Bennett**
Pg. 35   Ease: 3   Size: 8 $\frac{1}{2}$" x11" spread

Skill or Technique:
✔ intermediate journaling
✔ pocket page
✔ Sheldon logo used as frame
✔ Sheldon logo enlarged on copier and highlighted with gold gel marker
Supplies: Paper by Hallmark; Metallic Dots paper by Paper Pizazz; photo by Barlow Productions, Inc.; gel marker by Marvy; opaque gold marker by Zig

Figure 3-7—**Jupiter, Florida**
Pg. 36   Ease: 3   Size: 8 $\frac{1}{2}$" x11"

Skill or Technique:
✔ minimal journaling, capturing family correspondence
✔ using colored paper to make landforms
✔ using colored paper and markers to make water
✔ locator photo (a locator photo is a picture of a sign)
Supplies: Markers by Zig; Watercolour pencils by Derwent

Figure 3-8—**Fish Tales**
Pg. 37   Ease 2   Size: 8 $\frac{1}{2}$" x11" spread

Skill or Technique:
✔ intermediate journaling, using promotional copy
✔ using border paper
✔ trimming out designs from border
✔ punch art
✔ template lettering
✔ wave scissor detail and border
Supplies: Paper by Gibson Greeting; Lettering Template by Frances Meyer, Inc.; Wave design Paper Edgers by Fiskars

Figure 3-9—**The Summer of Doris**
Pg. 38   Ease: 3   Size: 8 $\frac{1}{2}$" x11"

Skill or Technique:
✔ extensive journaling, capturing a special memory
✔ using and changing stamp art
✔ using drop capital lettering on the computer (a drop capital occurs when the first letter of a word is enlarged and extends down into the copy area)
Supplies: Mother Bird stamp by Uptown Rubber Stamps; colored pencils by Berol; markers by Zig

Figure 3-10—**Gypsy**
Pg. 39   Ease: 3   Size: 8 $\frac{1}{2}$" x11"

Skill or Technique:
✔ extensive journaling, capturing a family story
✔ cropped photo
✔ use of shredded paper
Supplies: Paper by Frances Meyer, Inc.

Figure 3-11—**Charmed Life**
Pg. 40   Ease: 3   Size: 8 $\frac{1}{2}$" x11" spread

Skill or Technique:
✔ extensive journaling and editing
✔ photo by Kathleen Culbert-Aguilar
Supplies: White Satin paper by Paper Pizazz

Figure 4-2—**My Indiana Home**
Pg. 44   Ease: 3   Size: 12" x 12"

Skill or Technique:
✔ extensive journaling
✔ sweet peas are trimmed hearts punched out and rolled
✔ journaling on paper "sandwiches" with ribbon running through
Supplies: Paper by Keeping Memories Alive

Figure 4-8—**Animal Kingdom**
Pg. 50   Ease: 1   Size: 8 $\frac{1}{2}$" x11" spread

Skill or Technique:
✔ minimal journaling
✔ enlarged color photocopy from an ad
✔ ripped paper to form frame
Supplies: Lettering by Making Memories

Figure 5-1—**Kevin**
Pg. 54   Ease: 1   Size: 8 $\frac{1}{2}$" x11"

Skill or Technique:
✔ intermediate editing, using Internet source
✔ two kinds of mats
✔ trimming white border off of stickers
Supplies: Katie's Plaid paper by Provo Craft; stickers by Provo Craft; markers by Zig

Figure 7-2—**Kristine's Graduation**
Pg. 79   Ease: 2   Size: 8 ¹/₂" x11" spread

Skill or Technique:
✔ minimal journaling
✔ banner behind name
✔ using name for headline
Supplies: Sheet of Stars paper by Sonburn; markers by Zig

Figure 7-3—**Home for Christmas**
Pg. 80   Ease: 3   Size: 8 ¹/₂" x11"

Skill or Technique:
✔ minimal journaling
✔ pipe-cleaner wreaths
✔ punch art bows
✔ felt snow and headline lettering painted with fabric paint
✔ combining two photos to get the effect of one large tree
Supplies: Snowflakes paper by Paper Pizazz; Watercolour pencils by Derwent

Figure 7-4—**It's Your Birthday**
Pg. 81   Ease: 2   Size: 8 ¹/₂" x11"

Skill or Technique:
✔ minimal journaling of headlines and significant data only
✔ art from wrapping paper
✔ corner rounder used on only two corners
✔ silhouette cropping of dominant photo
✔ adding a crown
Supplies: Happy Birthday paper by Paper Pizazz

Figure 7-5—**Joseph Quinton**
Pg. 82   Ease: 3   Size: 8 ¹/₂" x11"

Skill or Technique:
✔ minimal journaling
✔ quilt made of squares of paper glued together in pattern
✔ punch art
✔ birth announcement card inside
Supplies: Paper by Paper Pizazz; Birthday Sprinkles paper by Provo Craft; Quilt lettering *The ABC's of Creative Lettering* by Lindsay Ostrom & Friends; marker by Zig

Figure 7-6—**Baby, Take a Bow**
Pg. 83   Ease: 2   Size: 8 ¹/₂" x11"

Skill or Technique:
✔ minimal journaling
✔ tile lettering using stars as tiles (tile lettering is the term used when you put a row of shapes behind the letters)
✔ star punch art used for journal border
✔ silver pen streaks
Supplies: Blue Stars paper by Paper Pizazz; opaque marker by Zig; blue marker by Marvy

Figure 7-7—**Brad Takes Off**
Pg. 84   Ease: 1   Size: 12" x12"

Skill or Technique:
✔ minimal journaling, copying Pilot's Flight Record, headline
✔ enlarged color copy of plane photo
✔ template lettering
✔ used striped background as border
✔ tilted 8 ¹/₂" x11" paper
Supplies: Cars and Planes paper by Paper Pizazz; Lettering Template by Frances Meyer, Inc.

Figure 7-9—**McDonald's**
Pg. 87   Ease: 2   Size: 8 ¹/₂" x11" spread

Skill or Technique:
✔ intermediate journaling
✔ stamped design made on paper with a potato stamp
Supplies: Special thanks to McDonald's Corporation for the paper supplies used

Figure 7-10—**Rams**
Pg. 88   Ease: 1   Size: 8 ¹/₂" x11"

Skill or Technique:
✔ intermediate journaling, captures activity
✔ football embellishments from wrapping paper
✔ stickers to match football embellishment
✔ lettering from office supply template
✔ sequencing of photos
Supplies: Football Field paper by Paper Pizazz; stickers by Mrs. Grossman's; markers by Zig

Figure 7-11—**Apple Picking**
Pg. 89   Ease: 2   Size: 12" x 12" spread

Skill or Technique:
✔ intermediate journaling
✔ using two different papers
✔ photojournaling with pictures
✔ some photos courtesy of Harry Ginsburg
Supplies: Green Honey Leaves by Provo Craft; Among Friends by Frances Meyer, Inc.; Edge Accents™ Scalloped scissors by Paper Adventures

Figure 8-1—**Herb Garden**
Pg. 92   Ease: 3   Size: 10" x 12"

Skill or Technique:
✔ minimal journaling of headline only
✔ border from 8 ¹/₂" x11" paper
✔ woven paper basket and paper frame
✔ dried plants embellishments
Supplies: Paper by Frances Meyer, Inc.; Swirl lettering from *The ABC's of Creative Lettering* by Lindsay Ostrom & Friends; markers by Zig

Figure 8-2—**Outdoor Education**
Pg. 93   Ease: 3   Size: 8 ¹/₂" x11" spread

Skill or Technique:
✔ extensive journaling, list made by child
✔ use of locator photo
✔ background paper made by enlarging and color copying a photo, cutting apart the copy with deckle edge scissors and piecing together a larger image
Supplies: Lettering template by Frances Meyer, Inc.; Deckle Paper Edgers by Fiskars

Figure 8-3—**Jungle Mike**
Pg. 94   Ease: 2   Size: 8 ¹/₂" x11"

Skill or Technique:
✔ intermediate journaling
✔ eye-directing path of hot pink paper
Supplies: Paper by Paper Adventures; lettering template by Frances Meyer, Inc.

Figure 8-4—**Easter Bunny**
Pg. 95   Ease: 1   Size: 8 ¹/₂" x11"

Skill or Technique:
✔ minimal journaling of headlines only
✔ felt bunny with features drawn with colored pencil and black marker
✔ Easter grass
✔ colored pencil used on basket
Supplies: Paper by Paper Pizazz; Swirls lettering from *The ABC's of Creative Lettering* by Lindsay Ostrom & Friends; markers by Zig

Figure 8-5—**Let It Snow**
Pg. 96   Ease: 2   Size: 8 ¹/₂" x11"

Skill or Technique:
✔ intermediate journaling
✔ free-hand snow lettering
✔ fancy scissor edging
✔ using designs from border paper as embellishments
✔ punch art pom-pom on hat
Supplies: Papers by Frances Meyer, Inc.; Pinking Paper Edgers by Fiskars

Figure 8-6—**Janie's Big Fish**
Pg. 97   Ease: 3   Size: 8 ¹/₂" x11" spread

Skill or Technique:
✔ extensive journaling of a family story
✔ heritage photos
Supplies: Fishing Time paper by Provo Craft; Pearlescent paper by Paper Pizazz; Mammoth Edge Accents™ scissors by Paper Adventures

*Figure 8-7—***Princess Green Beans**
Pg. 98   Ease: 3   Size: 8 ¹/₂" x11"
Skill or Technique:
✔ extensive journaling of a family memory, interviewing
✔ heritage page
✔ color copying of green beans can label
✔ enlarged art was sponge-painted
Supplies: Prudy's Pin Dot paper by Provo Craft; Swirl lettering by *The ABC's of Creative Lettering* by Lindsay Ostrom & Friends

*Figure 8-8—***Michael Scott**
Pg. 99   Ease: 2   Size: 8 ¹/₂" x11"
Skill or Technique:
✔ intermediate journaling and interview
✔ crimped paper
✔ scissor art of waves, boats and seagulls
Supplies: Paper by Hallmark; paper by Paper Patch; Wave Paper Edgers by Fiskars; Mammoth Edge Accents™ scissors by Paper Adventures

*Figure 8-9—***Friendship with Shirley**
Pg. 100-01 Ease: 3   Size: 8 ¹/₂" x11" spreads
Skill or Technique:
✔ extensive journaling and editing, use of quotations
✔ border from computer
✔ heritage page
Supplies: Paper by What's New?; Edge Accents™ and Mammoth Edge Accents™ Scalloped scissors by Paper Adventures; Scalloped edge oval punch by Family Treasures

*Figure 9-1—***Sisters**
Pg. 104   Ease: 1   Size: 8 ¹/₂" x11"
Skill or Technique:
✔ minimal journaling, capturing a poem and pertinent facts at a special event
✔ use of silk flowers
Supplies: Jewel Colors paper by Paper Pizazz; Carol's Script from *More than Memories*

*Figure 9-2—***Burger Queen**
Pg. 105   Ease: 3   Size: 8 ¹/₂" x11"
Skill or Technique:
✔ intermediate journaling, captures family memory
✔ creating stripes on paper by gluing down strips of paper
✔ using and altering die-cuts
✔ tile lettering with drop shadowing, handwritten head
✔ rick-rack trim made with scissors
✔ journaling on mat
Supplies: Sticker by Gibson Greetings; marker by Zig; Pinking Paper Edgers by Fiskars

*Figure 9-3—***Ketchup Sandwich**
Pg. 106   Ease: 2   Size: 8 ¹/₂" x11"
Skill or Technique:
✔ intermediate journaling, capturing family funny story and a child's likes/dislikes
✔ string attached to journaling element
✔ stamp art name
Supplies: Brown Corrugated Mix paper by Paper Pizazz; lettering from *The ABC's of Creative Lettering* by Lindsay Ostrom & Friends; marker by Zig; stickers by Sandy Lion

*Figure 9-4—***Indianapolis Dino**
Pg. 107   Ease: 2   Size: 8 ¹/₂" x11"
✔ intermediate journaling
✔ pocket for ticket
✔ dino by journaling traced from a piece of ribbon with dinosaurs on it
✔ computer lettering
Supplies: Paper by Paper Pizazz; Bubbles Paper Edgers by Fiskars

*Figure 9-5—***Over the Hill**
Pg. 108   Ease: 2   Size: 11" x 8 ¹/₂"
Skill or Technique:
✔ intermediate journaling
✔ sequencing of photos
✔ mixing textures of paper
Supplies: Marker by Zig; Red Silk paper by Hero Arts

*Figure 9-6—***Happy Birthday to Michael!**
Pg. 109   Ease: 2   Size: 8 ¹/₂" x11"
Skill or Technique:
✔ intermediate journaling
✔ deckle scissors used for ovals
✔ sticker lettering with mat to enlarge it
✔ fun with number "9" and photo
Supplies: Happy Birthday paper by Paper Pizazz; stickers by Mrs. Grossman's

*Figure 9-7—***Love Song**
Pg. 110   Ease: 3   Size: 8 ¹/₂" x11"
Skill or Technique:
✔ extensive journaling, saving a child's comments
✔ traced and colored in lettering
Supplies: Paper by Stamping Station; Stickers by Suzy's Zoo; colored pencils by Berol

*Figure 9-8—***Sweet William**
Pg. 111   Ease: 3   Size: 8 ¹/₂" x11"
Skill or Technique:
✔ intermediate journaling
✔ map from Internet
✔ use of punch art trees to make border (I know evergreens don't grow in Kenya, but these were the only trees I had!)
Supplies: Leaves Background paper by Design Originals; Puff lettering from *The ABC's of Creative Lettering* by Lindsay Ostrom & Friends; marker by Zig

*Figure 10-1—***Butterfly World**
Pg. 114   Ease: 3   Size: 8 ¹/₂" x11"
Skill or Technique:
✔ intermediate journaling
✔ pipe-cleaner antennae for insect
✔ headline matted and traced in black for emphasis
✔ photos fitted inside the wings
✔ template lettering
Supplies: Red Honey Checks paper by Provo Craft; lettering template by Frances Meyer, Inc.

*Figure 10-2—***Little Britches**
Pg. 115   Ease: 1   Size: 12" x12"
Skill or Technique:
✔ headline only
✔ using a corner punch
✔ using punches to create a theme
Supplies: Country Dots paper by Paper Pizazz; Lettering Template by Frances Meyer, Inc.; sample papers: Tri-dots on Lt. Blue paper by Paper Pizazz, Spatter and Bright Blue papers by Paperabilities III

*Figure 10-3—***Moods**
Pg. 116   special size
Supplies: Romantic papers by NRN Designs, Frances Meyer, Inc., and Paper Pizazz; Fun papers by Paper Patch and Paper Pizazz; Country papers by Paper Pizazz, unknown and Provo Craft; Classic papers by Gibson Greetings, Weedn Studios and Frances Meyer, Inc.; Romantic stamp by Uptown Rubber Stamps; Fun stamp by unknown and Stampendous!; Country stamp by PSX; Classic stamp by Rubber Stampede; Romantic sticker by Mrs. Grossman's; Fun stickers by Frances Meyer, Inc.; Country sticker by Provo Craft; Classic sticker by Frances Meyer, Inc.

Figure 10-4—**Daniéle Rose**
Pg. 117   Ease: 3   Size: 8 ½" x11"

Skill or Technique:
✔ minimal journaling
✔ thumbprint mats with trimmed out designs (thumbprints are my name for a protrusions on the inside of a mat)
✔ hand drawn rose
✔ purse opens and is lined in satin
Supplies: Peach Moire paper by Paper Pizazz; Tiny Roses paper by Design Originals; paper and lettering template Frances Meyer, Inc.

Figure 10-5—**Dino Mike**
Pg. 118   Ease: 3   Size: 8 ½" x11"
✔ minimal journaling
✔ using strips of bright paper and cutting out images for header
✔ silhouette mats
✔ template lettering
✔ triple mat headline
Supplies: Dinosaurs paper by Design Originals; Lettering Template by Frances Meyers, Inc.

Figure 10-6—**Prom**
Pg. 119   Ease: 1   Size: 8 ½" x11"
Skill or Technique:
✔ minimal journaling
✔ cutting paper to overlay headline
✔ using two "realistic papers"
Supplies: Paper by Paper Pizazz; Watercolour pencils by Derwent

Figure 10-7—**Picnic Poacher**
Pg. 120   Ease: 1   Size: 8 ½" x11"
Skill or Technique:
✔ minimal journaling, capturing correspondence and kid's comment
✔ unusual matting of large ant art
✔ free-hand lettering
Supplies: Paper by Frances Meyer, Inc.

Figure 10-8—**Chair of Bowlies**
Pg. 121   Ease: 3   Size: 8 ½" x11"
Skill or Technique:
✔ intermediate historic journaling
✔ dot and ball lettering
✔ drop shadowing of the mats (drop shadowing is intended to mimic the shadow that would occur if the item was lifted up off the page)
✔ colored pencil techniques on hat
✔ dotted paper made with gel pen
✔ punch art flowers and leaves
✔ heritage page
Supplies: Scatter Flowers paper by Provo Craft; colored pencils by Berol; markers by Marvy

Figure 10-9—**Mia**
Pg. 122   Ease: 3   Size: 8 ½" x11"

Skill or Technique:
✔ extensive journaling, letter to child
✔ ribbon woven through lace border
✔ pocket page
Supplies: Paper by Frances Meyer, Inc.; Paper by Paper Adventures

Figure 10-10—**Turtle Park**
Pg. 123   Ease: 3   Size: 8 ½" x11"
✔ minimal journaling
✔ puzzle page
Supplies: Markers by Zig

BONUS Figure—**Fortunate Family**
Pg. 124   Ease: 3   Size: 8 ½" x11"

Skill or Technique:
✔ minimal to extensive journaling
✔ interactive scrapbook and memory page
✔ background made by tracing Chinese food container art on light box
✔ lettering is a modification of a typestyle found in a clip art book
✔ gold seal is embossed stamp art
✔ hand-drawn fortune cookie
Supplies: Gold stripes by Mrs. Grossman's; stamp of sun by unknown; markers by Zig; colored pencils by Berol; gold pen by Marvy

Suppliers

Call these suppliers and ask for the retailer nearest you.

American Tombow, Inc.
(800) 835-3232
Mono®Adhesive is a registered trademark of American Tombow, Inc.

Amscan
(914) 345-2020; (800) 444-8887

Berol (Sanford Corporation)
(800) 323-0749

Chatterbox (Journaling Genies)
(208) 286-9517

Creating Keepsakes Magazine
(888) 247-5282; (801) 224-8235

Creative Card Company
(888) PAPERS2

Creative Photo Albums
DogByte Development
(800) 936-4298

Creative Memories
(800) 341-5275

Derwent
Rexel Limited
(800) REX-ART2

Design Originals
(800) 877-7820

Doumar Products
(888) buy-un-du; (972) 279-6633
un-du® is a registered trademark of
Doumar Products, Inc.

Family Treasures
(800) 413-2645; (805) 294-1330

Fiskars
(608) 233-1649

Flavia Publishing
(805) 564-6907

D.J. Inkers (Fontastic!)
(800) 325-4890

Frances Meyer, Inc.
(912) 748-5252

Gibson Greetings, Inc.
(513) 841-6600

Hallmark
(913) 727-6080

Hero Arts
(510) 652-6055

**Lindsay Ostrom & Friends
Cut-It-Up!**
ABC's of Creative Lettering
LMNOP: More Creative Lettering
(530) 389-2233

Lineco, Inc.
(413) 534-7204; (800) 322-7775

Keeping Memories Alive
(800) 419-4949

Making Memories
Memories, Inc.
(800) 929-7324

Magic American Corp.
(800) 321-6330
Goo Gone® is a registered trademark
of Magic American Corp.
Sticker Lifter™ is a trademark of Magic
American Corp.

Marvy
Uchida of America, Corp.
(800) 541-5877; (888) 666-5769

Memories Forever
Westrim Crafts
(800) 727-2727

Micron
Sakura of America
(800) 776-6257

More than Memories (book)
Edited by Julie Stephani
Krause Publications
(800) 258-0929

Mrs. Grossman's
(800) 429-4549; (707) 763-1700

NRN Design
(714) 898-6363; (800) 421-6958

Paper Adventures
(800) 727-0699
Edge Accents™ is a trademark of
Paper Adventures; Mammoth Edge
Accents™ is a trademark of Paper
Adventures

Paper Patch
(800) 397-2737; (801) 253-3018

Paper Pizazz
Hot Off The Press
(888) 326-7255

Paperabilities III
(800) 454-3331; (336) 861-6343

Provo Craft
(800) 563-8679 ; (800) 937-7686

PSX
Personal Stamp Exchange
(800) 782-6748

Rubber Stampede
(800) NEAT-FUN

Sandy Lion Stickers
(800) 461-6013

Sonburn, Inc.
(800) 527-7505

Stampa Rosa
(800) 554-5755; (707) 570-0763

Stampendous
(800) 869-0474; (714) 688-0288

Stamping Station
(800) 444-3828

Suzy's Zoo
(619) 452-9401

3M Scotch
(651) 733-1110
Post-It® is a registered trademark of 3M
Corporation

Uptown Rubber Stamps
(970) 493-3212

What's New?
(800) 272-3874

Weedn Studios
The Paper Center
Distributed by Gibson Paper to Kinko's
(800) 2-KINKOS

Zig
(800) 524-1349 ; (973) 458-0092

Find Scrapbook and Art Supplies In Your Area

In addition to calling the suppliers listed above, you can also find the retailers closest to you by seeing these online directories.

Graceful Bee
http://www.gracefulbee.com/
Includes: Yellow and White Page directories to retailers

Jangle
http://www.jangle.com/
Includes: Search directory to search by city, state and geographical distance

Scrapbooking Idea Network, The
http://scrapbooking.com
Includes: Local scrapbooking stores, workshops, groups, clubs, events and consultants

Ultimate Scrapbook Store Source
http://members.aol.com/kpenman617/Storelist.html
Includes: Retail store listings and links

Joanna's Top Book Picks

FOR JOURNALING:
The Art of Writing Scrapbook Stories
by Janice T. Dixon
Mount Olympus Pubs.
ISBN: 0965691977

FOR LETTERING
The ABC's of Creative Lettering
LMNOP More Creative Lettering
by Lindsay Ostrom & Friends

Handlettering for Decorative Artists
by Jackie O'Keefe
North Light Books
ISBN: 0-89134-825-5

The Scrapbooker's Book of Alphabets
by Melody Ross

GENERAL SCRAPBOOKING
A Lasting Legacy
by Souzzann Y. H. Carroll
Stellar Publishing
ISBN: 096633180X

All About Memory Albums
by Leisure Arts
ISBN: 1574860933

FOR DESIGN:
Core Composition
by Stacy Julian with Terina Darcey
Apple of Your Eye

Marvelous Scrapbook Makeovers
by Stacy Julian and Kate Johnson
Creating Keepsakes Magazine

FOR PUNCH ART
Punch Happy
by Tracey L. Isidro
Living Business Press
ISBN: 0966331818

Punchin'
by Suzanne McNeill

FOR STAMPING
The Complete Guide to Rubber Stamping
by Grace Taormina
Watson-Guptill Publications
ISBN: 0823046133

Decorating Scrapbooks with Rubber Stamps
by Dee Gruenig
Sterling Publications
ISBN: 0806998466

Creative Rubber Stamping Techniques
by MaryJo McGraw
North light Books
ISBN: 0-89134-878-6

MISCELLANEOUS:
Creating Family Newsletters
by Elaine Floyd
Newsletter Resources
ISBN: 0-9630222-7-X

Hand Coloring Black and White Photography
by Laurie Klein
A Quarry Book
ISBN: 1-56496-586-4

Making Memory Books by Hand
by Kristina Feliciano
A Quarry Book
ISBN: 1-56496-585-6

Index

Our goal is to make this book as useful as possible. To find where a subject is discussed, use the page numbers. To find where a subject is defined, turn to the page number given after *definition*. To see samples of techniques, use the Page Chart on page 125 to locate techniques and their page numbers.

Templates

Copy these templates on a black and white copier, enlarging or reducing the size as desired. Once you have a properly sized black and white copy, you can copy the template onto a clear overhead projector transparency. Cut out the template carefully with a craft knife. By putting the image on a transparency, you can see through the template which allows you to better position it as you use it. Overhead transparencies are available at your local office supply and copy shops.

Thank You!

This book could not have been written without the help of many, many people.

For sharing their knowledge of scrapbooking, thanks go to Margaret Campbell-Hutts, Amy Ginsburg (who also fed me and loaned me paper), Dawn Castillo and Lynne Cole. For helping me with supplies, trends, information and guidance, thanks go to Debra Winter of The Scrapbook Station (West Palm Beach, FL); Shirley Weiss and Sandi Rich of Memories Unlimited, Inc. (St. Louis, MO); Aimee Wright and Carol Hughes of Simply Scrapbooks (Parkville, MO); Tooti of Who-do-Knew? Art Stamp Outlet (Parkville, MO); the folks at All About Memories (O'Fallon, MO); the folks at Stamp Your Art Out (Orlando, FL); and the folks at The Scrapbook Cottage (Washington, MO). For sharing supplies with me I'd like to thank Karen Westover and Baudeville; and David Wilke and Paper Adventures.

For patiently guiding me through the process of color copying, I thank the people at Kinko's (Chesterfield, MO).

For supplying me with photos, thanks go to Harry Ginsburg (who was a great sport about this), Michael Scott, Joan Wojciechowski, Jenny Eickhorst, Mary Ellen Burford, Curt Hansen, Kathy Baker Moser, Sharla and Tom Zasadny, Pat Sonnett, Susan Lutz, Edward Manigault, Mari Pat and Patricia Varga, Michael Scott, Mary and Erin Vonesh, Elizabeth Burtelow, Brad Plumb, Nancy Nix-Rice, Elaine Todorov and the Sheldon Concert Hall and Ballroom.

For helping me keep my act together as a mother, wife and business owner, thanks go to Nadine Bailey, Irma Burmester, Sheila Jackson, Olivia Kormeier, Pat Sonnett and Pat and Erin Vonesh.

For helping with specific pages, I thank Peter Burmester and Dia, Grandma Marge and Sharon Bowman.

For design, graphics and photography thanks go to the Macintosh marvels at VIP Graphics. For fact-checking, indexing and online research, thanks go to Susan Todd at EFG.

For their support, enthusiasm and promotion of this project, thanks to the team at Betterway / Writer's Digest Books, especially Laura Smith and David Lewis.

Some folks deserve thanks for being such an important part of my life. Thanks to my sisters Jane Newell and Margaret Campbell-Hutts for giving birth to three adorable girls Alexandria (Lexie) Newell, Katigan and Makenna Hutts and one unforgettable little boy, Joshua David Newell. Thanks go to my mother Joanna Evans Funk Campbell for the loan of her memoirs and photos of her and Aunt Shirley Helmly. Thanks are due to Grandma Marge (Marjorie Parrott) for her angel encounter story and support in all my endeavors.

Last is not least. To David Slan go thanks for being my husband, partner and photo assistant. To Michael Slan go thanks for working on pages, helping me pick paper and supplies, posing for photos and being the wonderful guy he is. To Elaine Floyd go my heartfelt thanks for believing in me and being my forever friend.

This is NOT the end. It's just the beginning!

Let's keep in touch—Visit Joanna on her Web site
http://www.scrapbookstorytelling.com

At scrapbookstorytelling.com, you'll find new page ideas, tips and more! Plus, you'll be the first to know about Joanna's new products. Best of all, you'll be able to find out when Joanna is appearing at a scrapbooking store or speaking at an event near you.

The story continues... and you can be a part of it.